# Economics
## *A Free Market Reader*

Articles included in this book
appeared in the book titled:
FREE MARKET ECONOMICS: A BASIC READER
compiled by Bettina B. Greaves
and are reprinted here with the permission of
The Foundation for Economic Education
Irvington-on-Hudson, New York

Thought and Comprehension Questions
are original to this book and were written by
Jane A. Williams
and
Kathryn Daniels

published by
Bluestocking Press • Post Office Box 1014
Placerville • CA • 95667-1014
web site: www.BluestockingPress.com
Phone: 800-959-8586

Published by Bluestocking Press • P.O. Box 1014
Placerville, CA 95667-1014
web site: www.BluestockingPress.com

# Contents

# Publisher's Note

ECONOMICS: A FREE MARKET READER includes a selection of articles that originally appeared in THE FREEMAN, a monthly study journal published by The Foundation for Economic Education (FEE). The articles were originally compiled by Bettina Bien Greaves and reprinted in FREE MARKET ECONOMICS: A READER.

The articles that appear in this book were selected by Jane A. Williams, and are reprinted from FREE MARKET ECONOMICS: A READER with the permission of The Foundation for Economic Education, Inc. The questions appearing in this book have been contributed by Jane A. Williams and Kathryn Daniels and did not appear with the original articles.

For more information about free market economics, readers are encouraged to contact The Foundation for Economic Education.

Foundation for Economic Education
30 S. Broadway
Irvington-on-Hudson, NY 10533
Phone: (800) 960-4FEE
website: www.fee.org

# How to Use This Book

### WHAT DO YOU THINK?

Prior to each article is a shaded box containing "What Do You Think?" questions that should be answered based on the reader's current knowledge and/ or opinion of the topic. These questions should be answered *before* reading the article that follows each "What Do You Think?" section.

After answering the "What Do You Think?" questions, read the article that follows.

After reading the article, the reader should revisit his/her answers to the "What Do You Think?" questions to determine if the article has caused the reader to alter his/her thinking in any way. Why or why not?

### THOUGHT QUESTIONS

Complete the questions and/or exercises that follow each article in the section titled "Thought Questions." Thought questions are designed to facilitate student-teacher discussion. Comprehension questions are written to enhance the student's understanding and appreciation of the subject matter. Some questions and/or exercises may require research. Opinions should be supported with research, examples, reason, and/or logic.

## What Do You Think?

1. Define "political power."

2. Under what circumstances should government be permitted to use its power to force a citizen to do what the government wants the citizen to do, even if it's against the will of the individual citizen?

# A King of Long Ago[1]
by Lewis Love
*(for ages 12 and up)*

There once lived a king in a distant land—a just and wise old king, for he had observed and learned much about his people and about himself and his power. His people were free to go their way, and were fearful of the king and his soldiers, for his rule granted no privilege to one that was not a privilege to all equally. And they were free to petition their king and seek his wisdom in their affairs.

Thus there came one day to the royal court an artisan, a mason, and a beggar who was lame.

"O great and wise king," they cried, "we are sorely troubled with our plight."

---

[1] From ROTAGRAPH, March 16, 1962 (Fort Worth, Texas, Rotary Club). Reprinted from THE FREEMAN, July 1962. Reprinted with permission of the Foundation for Economic Education, 30 S. Broadway, Irvington-on-Hudson, NY.

"I," said the artisan, "make many useful goods. I use great skill and labor long, and yet when I am finished, the people will not pay my price."

"And I," said the mason, "am a layer of stone for houses and fine walls, yet I am idle, for no one gives me work."

"I am a poor lame beggar," said the third man, "who seeks alms from those who pass, as they find it in their hearts to do so, but alms are so few as to be of great concern lest I perish."

"I can see that your trouble is great," consoled the king, "and what would you ask of me?"

Then, they spoke as a group, the artisan, the mason, and the beggar who was lame: "Your power is very great, our king, and you can make the people see the folly of their ways and aid us in our troubles."

> **Before reading further, answer Thought Question #1 at the end of this story. After answering Question #1, continue reading "A King of Long Ago."**

"Perhaps," said the king, "perhaps my power is great, but I must use it wisely or it shall be lost." And he called to the captain of his guard.

"Bring forth three swords," he commanded, "one for each of these men, and instruct them in their use. These three shall go forth in the land and compel those who will not voluntarily deal with them to obey their command."

"No! No!" the three men called out, "this we did not ask. We are men of honor and could not set upon our fellow man to compel him to our will. This we cannot do. It is you, O king, who must use the power."

"You ask me to do that which you would not do because of honor?" questioned the king. "Is honor one thing to a beggar and another to a king? I, too, am an honorable man, and that which is dishonorable for you will never be less dishonorable for your king."

# Thought Questions

1.  If you were the king, what would be your response to the artisan, the mason, and the beggar when they said, "Your power is very great, our king, and you can make the people see the folly of their ways and aid us in our troubles"?

2.  Now that you have finished reading "A King of Long Ago," would you change your answer to Question #1, listed above; and if so, how; if not, why not?

3.  The king asks, "Is honor one thing to a beggar and another to a king?" Do you think every person, whether a king or peasant, should be subject to the same rules and the same code of honor? Explain your answer. List examples from history in which a government leader behaved in a fashion that was dishonorable (i.e. kings, presidents, prime ministers).

4.  Lord Acton stated in LORD ACTON: LETTER TO BISHOP MANDELL CREIGHTON [1887], "Power tends to corrupt; absolute power corrupts absolutely." Do you agree or disagree with this statement? Explain your answer. Supply examples to support your position.

5.  "Your power is very great, our king, and you can make the people see the folly of their ways and aid us in our troubles." The three men are asking the king to use a king's power to force people to aid the three men. Explain how their request differs from the request of individuals, special interest groups, and lobbyists who ask senators and representatives to pass legislation that will favor some, but not others. If a law is passed, and an individual chooses

not to obey the law, what might be the consequences to that
individual in today's society? Provide examples to support your
position.

6.     Can you think of any circumstances in which one person or group
       should be granted privileges that should not be granted to
       everyone? What might be the consequences of such action?

7.     If you were excluded from a privilege granted by a king or other
       ruler, how would you react? What might be your position towards
       the person/s who granted the privilege? What might be your
       position towards the person/s who received the privilege?

8.     If you have siblings, can you think of any situation/s in which
       your sibling was granted a privilege by a parent that you were not
       granted? How did that make you feel: towards the sibling? towards
       the parent?

9.     Explain how the artisan, mason, and beggar might solve their own
       problems without the intervention of the king's use of power.

10.    Richard Maybury, author of WHATEVER HAPPENED TO PENNY CANDY?
       defines political power as "the legal privilege of using force on
       persons who have not harmed anyone. [Political power is] the
       legal privilege of backing one's decisions with violence or threats
       of violence." Do you agree or disagree with Maybury's definition
       of political power and why? List examples to support your
       position.

## What Do You Think?

1.  Government spends money. From where does the money come that government spends?

2.  If you were forming a new government, would you tax people? If so, what would you do with the tax money you received?

3.  What services do you believe government should provide, and what services should be provided by private companies?

4.  Do you believe in a strict interpretation of the Constitution or a liberal interpretation of the Constitution? Explain your answer.

# Not Yours to Give[2]

### by David Crockett

*(for ages 14 and up)*

One day in the House of Representatives, a bill was taken up appropriating money for the benefit of a widow of a distinguished naval officer. Several beautiful speeches had been made in its support. The Speaker was just about to put the question when Crockett arose:

---

[2] From THE LIFE OF COLONEL DAVID CROCKETT, compiled by Edward S. Ellis (Philadelphia: Porter & Coates, 1884). Reprinted with permission of the Foundation for Economic Education, 30 S. Broadway, Irvington-on-Hudson, NY.

"Mr. Speaker—I have as much respect for the memory of the deceased, and as much sympathy for the sufferings of the living, if suffering there be, as any man in this House, but we must not permit our respect for the dead or our sympathy for a part of the living to lead us into an act of injustice to the balance of the living. I will not go into an argument to prove that Congress has no power to appropriate this money as an act of charity. Every member upon this floor knows it. We have the right, as individuals, to give away as much of our own money as we please in charity; but as members of Congress we have no right so to appropriate a dollar of the public money. Some eloquent appeals have been made to us upon the ground that it is a debt due the deceased. Mr. Speaker, the deceased lived long after the close of the war; he was in office to the day of his death, and I have never heard that the government was in arrears to him.

"Every man in this House knows it is not a debt. We cannot, without the grossest corruption, appropriate this money as the payment of a debt. We have not the semblance of authority to appropriate it as charity. Mr. Speaker, I have said we have the right to give as much money of our own as we please. I am the poorest man on this floor. I cannot vote for this bill, but I will give one week's pay to the object, and if every member of Congress will do the same, it will amount to more than the bill asks."

He took his seat. Nobody replied. The bill was put upon its passage, and, instead of passing unanimously, as was generally supposed, and as, no doubt, it would, but for that speech, it received but few votes, and, of course, was lost.

Later, when asked by a friend why he had opposed the appropriation, Crockett gave this explanation:

"Several years ago I was one evening standing on the steps of the Capitol with some other members of Congress, when our attention was attracted by a great light over in Georgetown. It was evidently a large fire. We jumped into a hack and drove over as fast as we could. In spite of all that could be done, many houses were burned and many families made houseless, and, besides, some of them had lost all but the clothes they had on. The weather was very cold, and when I saw so many women and children suffering, I felt that something ought to be done for them. The next morning a bill was introduced appropriating $20,000 for their relief. We put aside all other business and rushed it through as soon as it could be done.

"The next summer, when it began to be time to think about the election, I concluded I would take a scout around among the boys of my district. I had no opposition there, but, as the election was some time off, I did not know what might turn up. When riding one day in a part of my district in which I was more of a stranger than any other, I saw a man in a field plowing and coming toward the road. I gauged my gait so that we should meet as he came to the fence. As he came up, I spoke to the man. He replied politely, but, as I thought, rather coldly.

"I began: 'Well, friend, I am one of those unfortunate beings called candidates, and—'

" 'Yes, I know you; you are Colonel Crockett. I have seen you once before, and voted for you the last time you were elected. I suppose you are out electioneering now, but you had better not waste your time or mine. I shall not vote for you again.'

"This was a sockdolager . . . I begged him to tell me what was the matter.

" 'Well, Colonel, it is hardly worthwhile to waste time or words upon it. I do not see how it can be mended, but you gave a vote last winter which shows that either you have not capacity to understand the Constitution, or that you are wanting in the honesty and firmness to be guided by it. In either case you are not the man to represent me. But I beg your pardon for expressing it in that way. I did not intend to avail myself of the privilege of the constituent to speak plainly to a candidate for the purpose of insulting or wounding you. I intend by it only to say that your understanding of the Constitution is very different from mine; and I will say to you what, but for my rudeness, I should not have said, that I believe you to be honest . . . . But an understanding of the Constitution different from mine I cannot overlook, because the Constitution, to be worth anything, must be held sacred, and rigidly observed in all its provisions. The man who wields power and misinterprets it is the more dangerous the more honest he is.'

" 'I admit the truth of all you say, but there must be some mistake about it, for I do not remember that I gave any vote last winter upon any constitutional question.'

" 'No, Colonel, there's no mistake. Though I live here in the backwoods and seldom go from home, I take the papers from Washington and read very carefully all the proceedings of Congress. My papers say that last winter you voted for a bill to appropriate $20,000 to some sufferers by a fire in Georgetown. Is that true?'

" 'Well, my friend; I may as well own up. You have got me there. But certainly nobody will complain that a great and rich country like ours should give the insignificant sum of $20,000 to relieve its suffering women and children, particularly with a full and overflowing Treasury, and I am sure, if you had been there, you would have done just as I did.'

" 'It is not the amount, Colonel, that I complain of; it is the principle. In the first place, the government ought to have in the Treasury no more than enough for its legitimate purposes. But that has nothing to do with the question. The power of collecting and disbursing money at pleasure is the most dangerous power that can be intrusted to man, particularly under our system of collecting revenue by a tariff, which reaches every man in the country, no matter how poor he may be, and the poorer he is the more he pays in proportion to his means. What is worse, it presses upon him without his knowledge where the weight centers, for there is not a man in the United States who can ever guess how much he pays to the government. So you see, that while you are contributing to relieve one, you are drawing it from thousands who are even worse off than he. If you had the right to give anything, the amount was simply a matter of discretion with you, and you had as much right to give $20,000,000 as $20,000. If you have the right to give to one, you have the right to give to all; and, as the Constitution neither defines charity nor stipulates the amount, you are at liberty to give to any and everything which you may believe, or profess to believe, is a charity, and to any amount you may think proper. You will very easily perceive what a wide door this would open for fraud and corruption and favoritism, on the one hand, and for robbing the people on the other. No, Colonel, Congress has no right to give charity. Individual members may give as much of their own money as they please, but they have no right to touch a dollar of the public money for that purpose. If twice as many houses had been burned in this county as in Georgetown, neither you nor any other member of Congress would have thought of appropriating a dollar for our relief. There are about two hundred and forty members of Congress. If they had shown their sympathy for the sufferers by contributing each one week's pay, it would have made over $13,000. There are plenty of wealthy men in and around

Washington who could have given $20,000 without depriving themselves of even a luxury of life. The congressmen chose to keep their own money, which, if reports be true, some of them spend not very creditably; and the people about Washington, no doubt, applauded you for relieving them from the necessity of giving by giving what was not yours to give. The people have delegated to Congress, by the Constitution, the power to do certain things. To do these, it is authorized to collect and pay moneys, and for nothing else. Everything beyond this is usurpation, and a violation of the Constitution.'

" 'So you see, Colonel, you have violated the Constitution in what I consider a vital point. It is a precedent fraught with danger to the country, for when Congress once begins to stretch its power beyond the limits of the Constitution, there is no limit to it, and no security for the people. I have no doubt you acted honestly, but that does not make it any better, except as far as you are personally concerned, and you see that I cannot vote for you.'

"I tell you I felt streaked. I saw if I should have opposition, and this man should go to talking, he would set others to talking, and in that district I was a gone fawn-skin. I could not answer him, and the fact is, I was so fully convinced that he was right, I did not want to. But I must satisfy him, and I said to him:

" 'Well, my friend, you hit the nail upon the head when you said I had not sense enough to understand the Constitution. I intended to be guided by it, and thought I had studied it fully. I have heard many speeches in Congress about the powers of Congress, but what you have said here at your plow has got more hard, sound sense in it than all the fine speeches I ever heard. If I had ever taken the view of it that you have, I would have put my head into the fire before I would have given that vote; and if you will forgive me and vote for me again, if I ever vote for another unconstitutional law I wish I may be shot.'

"He laughingly replied: 'Yes, Colonel, you have sworn to that once before, but I will trust you again upon one condition. You say that you are convinced that your vote was wrong. Your acknowledgment of it will do more good than beating you for it. If, as you go around the district, you will tell people about this vote, and that you are satisfied it was wrong, I will not only vote for you, but will do what I can to keep down opposition, and, perhaps, I may exert some little influence in that way.'

" 'If I don't,' said I, 'I wish I may be shot; and to convince you that I am in earnest in what I say I will come back this way in a week or ten days, and if you will get up a gathering of the people, I will make a speech to them. Get up a barbecue, and I will pay for it.'

" 'No, Colonel, we are not rich people in this section, but we have plenty of provisions to contribute for a barbecue, and some to spare for those who have none. The push of crops will be over in a few days, and we can then afford a day for a barbecue. This is Thursday; I will see to getting it up on Saturday week. Come to my house on Friday, and we will go together, and I promise you a very respectable crowd to see and hear you.'

" 'Well, I will be here. But one thing more before I say good-by. I must know your name.'

" 'My name is Bunce.'

" 'Not Horatio Bunce?'

" 'Yes.'

" 'Well, Mr. Bunce, I never saw you before, though you say you have seen me, but I know you very well. I am glad I have met you, and very proud that I may hope to have you for my friend.'

"It was one of the luckiest hits of my life that I met him. He mingled but little with the public, but was widely known for his remarkable intelligence and incorruptible integrity, and for a heart brimful and running over with kindness and benevolence, which showed themselves not only in words but in acts. He was the oracle of the whole country around him, and his fame had extended far beyond the circle of his immediate acquaintance. Though I had never met him before, I had heard much of him, and but for this meeting it is very likely I should have had opposition, and had been beaten. One thing is very certain, no man could now stand up in that district under such a vote.

"At the appointed time I was at his house, having told our conversation to every crowd I had met, and to every man I stayed all night with, and I found that it gave the people an interest and a confidence in me stronger than I had ever seen manifested before.

"Though I was considerably fatigued when I reached his house, and, under ordinary circumstances, should have gone early to bed, I kept him up until midnight, talking about the principles and affairs of government, and got more real, true knowledge of them than I had got all my life before.

"I have known and seen much of him since, for I respect him—no, that is not the word—I reverence and love him more than any living man, and I go to see him two or three times every year; and I will tell you, sir, if every one who professes to be a Christian lived and acted and enjoyed it as he does, the religion of Christ would take the world by storm.

"But to return to my story. The next morning we went to the barbecue, and, to my surprise, found about a thousand men there. I met a good many whom I had not known before, and they and my friend introduced me around until I had got pretty well acquainted—at least, they all knew me.

"In due time notice was given that I would speak to them. They gathered up around a stand that had been erected. I opened my speech by saying:

" 'Fellow-citizens—I present myself before you today feeling like a new man. My eyes have lately been opened to truths which ignorance or prejudice, or both, had heretofore hidden from my view. I feel that I can today offer you the ability to render you more valuable service than I have ever been able to render before. I am here today more for the purpose of acknowledging my error than to seek your votes. That I should make this acknowledgment is due to myself as well as to you. Whether you will vote for me is a matter for your consideration only.'

"I went on to tell them about the fire and my vote for the appropriation and then told them why I was satisfied it was wrong. I closed by saying:

" 'And now, fellow-citizens, it remains only for me to tell you that the most of the speech you have listened to with so much interest was simply a repetition of the arguments by which your neighbor, Mr. Bunce, convinced me of my error.

" 'It is the best speech I ever made in my life, but he is entitled to the credit for it. And now I hope he is satisfied with his convert and that he will get up here and tell you so.'

"He came upon the stand and said:

" 'Fellow-citizens—It affords me great pleasure to comply with the request of Colonel Crockett. I have always considered him a thoroughly honest man, and I am satisfied that he will faithfully perform all that he has promised you today.'

"He went down, and there went up from that crowd such a shout for Davy Crockett as his name never called forth before.

"I am not much given to tears, but I was taken with a choking then and felt some big drops rolling down my cheeks.

And I tell you now that the remembrance of those few words spoken by such a man, and the honest, hearty shout they produced, is worth more to me than all the honors I have received and all the reputation I have ever made, or ever shall make, as a member of Congress.

"Now, sir," concluded Crockett, "you know why I made that speech yesterday.

"There is one thing now to which I will call your attention. You remember that I proposed to give a week's pay. There are in that House many very wealthy men—men who think nothing of spending a week's pay, or a dozen of them, for a dinner or a wine party when they have something to accomplish by it. Some of those same men made beautiful speeches upon the great debt of gratitude which the country owed the deceased—a debt which could not be paid by money—and the insignificance and worthlessness of money, particularly so insignificant a sum as $10,000 when weighed against the honor of the nation. Yet not one of them responded to my proposition. Money with them is nothing but trash when it is to come out of the people. But it is the one great thing for which most of them are striving, and many of them sacrifice honor, integrity, and justice to obtain it."

# Thought Questions

1.  Define the word "charity." What provision in the U.S. Constitution permits Congress to spend other people's money for charity?

2.  Davy Crockett states, "We must not permit our respect for the dead or our sympathy for a part of the living to lead us into an act of injustice to the balance of the living. . . We have the right, as individuals, to give away as much of our own money as we please in charity; but as members of Congress we have no right so to

appropriate a dollar of the public money." Do you agree or disagree that public funds should not be used for acts of charity? How do you think Davy Crockett would respond to the current use of public funds for disaster relief? [relief for victims of: hurricanes, floods, earthquake, war at both home and abroad, etc.]

3.      Read the article "Government and Disaster Relief," from the September 1997 issue of THE FREEMAN that is posted (at the time of this writing) at website: www.libertyhaven.com/noneoftheabove/ disasters/govdisasters.html. Would Horatio Bunce have agreed or disagreed with author Lawrence W. Reed? Explain.

4.      Currently when a large disaster occurs in the U.S., the Federal government grants Federal disaster relief. Following the 1906 San Francisco Earthquake the following comments appeared in an article printed in HARPER'S WEEKLY NEWSPAPER on May 12, 1906. According to the following article, who will rebuild San Francisco?

> Some surprise and concern seem to have been caused in San Francisco by the discovery that of the $2,500,000 appropriated by Congress for the inhabitants of the stricken city, only about $300,000 will reach them in the shape of cash. They overlook the fact that the appropriation had to be used primarily to make good the rations and other supplies furnished by the military and naval authorities. Neither Secretary Taft nor Secretary Bonaparte had a right to expend a dollar or a dollar's worth of supplies for the purpose of relieving the necessities of the victims of the catastrophe, though they rightly dealt with an awful emergency on the assumption that their acts would be ratified by Congress. The ratification came promptly, but it must be remembered that it took the form of specifying $2,500,000 as the outlay beyond which the war Department and the Navy Department must not go. No doubt a considerable proportion of the private contributions has also been disbursed and local committees in San Francisco and other afflicted towns in California will, nevertheless, be large. The funds needed for reconstruction, however, will, of course, come mainly from the fire-insurance companies and from capitalists who are willing to erect new buildings

on their own lands or to make building loans on the lands of others.

— HARPER'S WEEKLY NEWSPAPER
May 12, 1906

5.      What does the term "sockdolager" mean?

6.      Horatio Bunce says to Davy Crockett, ". . . your understanding of the Constitution is very different from mine; and I will say to you what, but for my rudeness, I should not have said, that I believe you to be honest . . . But an understanding of the Constitution different from mine I cannot overlook, because the Constitution, to be worth anything, must be held sacred, and rigidly observed in all its provisions. The man who wields power and misinterprets it is the more dangerous the more honest he is." Do you agree or disagree with Mr. Bunce? Explain your answer.

7.      Horatio Bunce observes, "The power of collecting and disbursing money at pleasure is the most dangerous power that can be intrusted to man, particularly under our system of collecting revenue by a tariff, which reaches every man in the country, no matter how poor he may be." Why does Mr. Bunce consider this power dangerous and do you agree or disagree?

8.      Mr. Bunce states to Davy Crockett that "when Congress once begins to stretch its power beyond the limits of the Constitution, there is no limit to it, and no security for the people." Do you agree or disagree and why?

9.      For research: What additional information can you find regarding Horatio Bunce?

10.     Davy Crockett said about his fellow members of Congress, "Money with them is nothing but trash when it is to come out of the people. But it is the one great thing for which most of them are striving, and many of them sacrifice honor, integrity, and justice to obtain it." For the next few months, keep a list of anything that is proposed, enacted into law, or administrated that will require taxpayers' money for what Horatio Bunce would have classified as "charity".

## What Do You Think?

1. Does more money create greater prosperity? Explain.

2. From where does the money come that government uses to fund its programs?

3. What do business people do when they have more products to sell than customers who are willing to buy at the asking price?

# How Much Money?[3]
by Percy L. Greaves, Jr.
*(for ages 15 and up)*

Most people want more money. So do I. But I wouldn't keep it long. I would soon spend it for the things I need or want. So would most people. In other words, for most of us, more money is merely a means for buying what we really want. Only misers want more money for the sake of holding onto it permanently.

However, if more money is to be given out, most of us would like to get some of it. If we can't get any for ourselves, the next best thing, from our viewpoint, would be for it to be given to those who might buy our goods or services. For then it is likely their increased spending would make us richer.

---

[3] From THE FREEMAN, May 1965. Reprinted with permission of the Foundation for Economic Education, 30 S. Broadway, Irvington-on-Hudson, NY.

From such reasoning, many have come to believe that spreading more money around is a good thing—not only for their personal needs, but also for solving most all of the nation's problems. For them, more money becomes the source of prosperity. So they approve all sorts of government programs for pumping more money into the economy.

If such programs are helpful, why not have more money for everyone? Why not have the government create and give everyone $100 or $200 or, better yet, $1,000? Why not have the government do it every year or every month or, better yet, every week?

Of course, such a system would not work. But why not? When we understand why not, we will know why every attempt to create prosperity by creating more money will not work. When we have learned the answer, we shall have taken a long step toward eliminating the greatest cause of both human misery and the decay of great civilizations.

One way to find the answer is to analyze the logic which seemingly supports the idea that more money in a nation's economy means more prosperity for all. If we can spot an error in the chain of reasoning, we should be able to make it clear to others. Once such an error is generally recognized, the popularity of government money-creation programs will soon disappear. Neither moral leaders nor voting majorities will long endorse ideas they know to be false.

Perhaps the basic thought that supports an ever-increasing money supply is the popular idea that more business requires more money: if we produce more goods and services, customers must have more money with which to buy the additional goods and services. From this, it is assumed that the need for prosperity and "economic growth" makes it the government's duty to pump out more purchasing power to the politically worthy in the form of more money or subsidies paid for by the creation of more money.

Support for such reasoning is found in an idea that goes back at least to medieval days. In the thirteenth and fourteenth centuries some of the world's best minds believed there was a "just price" for everything. The "just price" was then thought to be determined by a fixed cost of production. Actual prices might fluctuate slightly from day to day or season to season, but they were always expected to return to the basic "just price," reflecting the supposedly never-changing number of man-hours required for production.

From such thinking, it naturally follows that increased production can only be sold when consumers have more money. More goods might be needed for any of several reasons, let us say for an increased population. However, no matter how much they were needed, they would remain unsold and unused unless buyers were supplied additional funds with which to buy them at, or near, the "just price."

What is the situation in real life? What do businessmen do when they have more goods to sell than customers will buy at their asking price?

They reduce prices. They advertise sales at mark-down prices. If that doesn't work, they reduce their prices again and again until all their surplus goods are sold. Any economic good can always be sold, if the price is right.

The way to move increased production into consumption is to adjust prices downward. Businessmen, who have made mistakes in judging consumer wants, will suffer losses. Those who provide what consumers prefer will earn profits. Lower prices will benefit all consumers and mean lower costs for future business operations. Under such a flexible price system, there is no need for more money. Businessmen soon learn to convert available supplies of labor and raw materials into those goods for which consumers will willingly pay the highest prices.

## What Are Prices?

Prices are quantities of money. They reflect a complex of interrelated market conditions and individual value judgments at any one time and place. Each price reflects not only the available supply of that good in relation to the supply of all other available goods and services, but also the demand of individuals for that good in relation to their demand for all other available goods and services.

But even this is only one side of price-determining factors. The money side must also be taken into consideration. Every price also reflects not only the supply of money held by each market participant, but also—since very few people ever spend their last cent—how much money each participant decides to keep for his future needs and unknown contingencies.

Prices thus depend on many things besides the cost of production. They depend primarily on the relative values that consumers place on the satisfactions they expect to get from owning the particular mixture of goods and services that they select. However, prices also depend on the amount of money available both to each individual and to all individuals. In a free market economy, unhampered prices easily adjust to reflect consumer demand no matter what the total supply of money or who owns how much of it.

## What is This Thing Called Money?

Money is a commodity that is used for facilitating indirect exchange. Money first appeared when individuals recognized the advantages of the division of labor and saw that indirect exchange was easier and more efficient than the clumsy, time-consuming direct exchange of barter.

In the earliest days of specialized production, those who made shoes or caught fish soon found that if they wanted to buy a house, it was easier to buy it with a quantity of a universally desired commodity than with quantities of shoes or fresh fish.

So, they first exchanged their shoes or fish for a quantity of that commodity which they knew was most in demand. Such a commodity would keep and not spoil. It could be divided without loss. And most important, all people would value it no matter what the size of their feet or their desire for fish. The commodity which best meets these qualifications soon becomes a community's medium of exchange, or money.

Many things have been used as money. In this country we once used the wampum beads of Indians and the shells found on our shores. As time passed, reason and experience indicated that the commodities best suited for use as money were the precious metals, silver and gold. By the beginning of this century, the prime money of the world had become gold. And so it is today. Gold is the commodity most in demand in world markets.

Money is always that commodity which all sellers are most happy to accept for their goods or services, if the quantity or price offered is considered sufficient. Money is thus the most marketable commodity of a market society. It is also the most important single commodity of a market society. This is so because it forms a part of every market transaction and whatever affects its value affects every transaction and every contemplated transaction.

## Kinds of Goods

There are three types of economic goods:

1. Consumers' goods.
2. Producers' goods.
3. Money.

Consumers' goods are those goods which are valued because they supply satisfaction to those who use or consume them. Producers' goods are goods which are valued because they can be used to make or produce consumers' goods. They include raw materials, tools, machines, factories, railroads, and the like. Money is that good which is valued because it can be used as a medium of exchange. It is the only type of economic good that is not consumed by its normal usage.

In the case of consumers' goods and producers' goods, every additional unit that is produced and offered for sale increases the wealth not only of the owner but of everyone else. Every additional automobile that is produced not only makes the manufacturer richer but it also makes every member of the market society richer.

How?

The more useful things there are in this world, the larger the numbers of human needs or wants that can be satisfied. The market system is a process for distributing a part of every increase in production to every participant in that market economy. When there is no increase in the money supply, the more goods that are offered for sale, the lower prices will be—and, consequently, the more each person can buy with the limited amount of money he has to spend. So every increase in production for a market economy normally means more for every member of that economy.

On the other hand, when any consumers' goods or producers' goods are lost or destroyed, not only the owner but all members of the market community suffer losses. With fewer goods available in the market place, and assuming no increase in the money supply, prices must tend to rise. Everybody's limited supply of money will thus buy less.

Recently, a Montreal apartment house was destroyed by an explosion. The loss to the occupants and the owners or insurance companies is obvious. The loss to all of us may be less obvious, but nevertheless it is a fact.

The market society has lost forever the services and contributions of all those who were killed. It has also lost for a time the contributions of all those whose injuries temporarily incapacitated them. There is also a loss for all of us in the fact that human services and producers' goods must be used to clear away the wreckage and rebuild what was destroyed. This diversion of labor and producers' goods means the market will never be able to offer the things that such labor and producers' goods could otherwise have been used to produce. With fewer things available in the market, prices will tend to be higher. Such higher prices will force each one of us to get along with a little less than would have been the case if there had been no explosion.

Thus, we are all sufferers from every catastrophe. Be it an airplane crash, a tornado, or a fire in some distant community, we all lose a little bit. And all these little bits often add up to a significant sum.

This is particularly true of war losses. Every American killed in Vietnam hurts every one of us not only in the heart but also in the pocketbook. Our government must supply some monetary compensation to his family and an income, however little, to his dependents. In such cases, the loss may continue for years. The killed man's services are lost for his normal life span and his dependents become a long-term burden on the nation's taxpayers and consumers. Such losses can never be measured or calculated, but they are real nonetheless.

So, in a market society every increase in consumers' goods or producers' goods permits us to buy more with whatever money we have, and every decrease in consumers' goods or producers' goods means ultimately higher prices and less for our money. Increased supplies of such economic goods help both the producers and everyone else who owns one or more units of money. *Stop*

## Limited Goods Available

With money, the situation is quite different. Any increase in the supply of money helps those who receive some of the new supply, but it hurts all those who do not. Those who receive some of the new supply can rush out and buy a larger share of the goods and services in the market place. Those who receive none of the new money supply will then find less available for them to buy. Prices will rise and they will get less for their money.

Pumping more money into a nation's economy merely helps some people at the expense of others. It must, by its very nature, send prices up higher than they would have been, if the money supply had not been increased. Those with no part of the new money supply must be satisfied with less. It does not and cannot increase the quantity of goods and services available.

There are some who claim that increasing the money supply puts more men to work. This can only be so when there is unemployment resulting from pushing wage rates above those of a free market by such political measures as minimum wage laws and legally sanctioned labor union pressures. Under such conditions, increasing the money supply reduces the value of each monetary unit and thus reduces the real value of all wages. By doing this, it brings the higher-than-free-market wage rates nearer to what they would be in a free market. This in turn brings employment nearer to what it would be in a free market, where there is a job for all who want to work.[4]

Those who create and slip new supplies of money into the economy are silently transferring wealth which rightfully belongs to savers and producers to those who, without contributing to society, are the first to spend the new money in the market place. When this is done by private persons, they are called counterfeiters. Their attempts to help themselves at the expense of others are easily recognized. When caught, they are soon placed where they can add no more to the money supply.

In recent generations our major problem has not been private counterfeiters. It has been governments. Over the years, governments have found ways to increase the money supply that not more than one or two persons in a million can detect. This is particularly true when production is increasing and when more and more of the monetary units are held off the market. Nonetheless, whether prices go up or not, every time a government increases the money supply, it is taking wealth from some and giving it to others.

This semi-hidden increase in the money supply occurs in two ways:

---

[4] See "Jobs for All" by Percy L. Greaves, Jr., (pg 83 of this book).

One, by the creation and issuance of money against government securities. This is a favorite way to finance government deficits. Government securities that private investors will not buy, because they pay lower-than-free-market interest rates, are sold to commercial banks. The banks pay for such securities by merely adding the price of the securities to government bank accounts. The government can then draw checks to pay suppliers, employees, and subsidy recipients. (This process is encouraged and increased by technical actions and direct purchases of the nation's central bank. In the United States, these powers reside in the Federal Reserve Board, which has not been hesitant about using them.)

The government thus receives purchasing power without contributing anything to the goods and services offered in the market place. It thus gets something for nothing. As a result, there is less available for those spending and investing dollars they have received for their contributions to society. The consequence of such government spending is that prices are higher than they would otherwise have been.

Two, the other major semi-hidden means of increasing the money supply is for banks to lend money to private individuals or organizations by merely creating or adding a credit to the borrowers' checking accounts. In such cases, they are not lending the savings of depositors. They are merely creating dollars, in the form of bank accounts, by simple bookkeeping entries. The borrowers are thereby enabled to draw checks or ask for newly created money with which to buy a part of the goods and services available in the market place. This means that those responsible for the production of these goods and services must be satisfied with less than the share they would have received if the money supply had not been so increased.

By such systems of money creation, our government and our government-controlled banking system have, from the end of 1945, increased the nation's money supply from $132.5 billion to an estimated $289.9 billion by the end of 1964. This is an increase of $157.4 billion. During the same period, the gold stock, held as a reserve against this money and valued at $35 an ounce, fell from $20.1 billion to $15.4 billion. The increase in the money supply for 1964 amounted to $21.0 billion.[5]

All these new dollars provided the first recipients with wealth which, had there been no artificial additions to the money supply, would have gone to those spenders and investors who received their dollars in return for contributions to society. Last year alone, political favorites were helped to the tune of $21 billion, at the expense of all the nation's producers and savers of real wealth.

These money-increasing policies remain hidden from most people, particularly when prices do not rise rapidly. It is now popular to say there is no inflation unless official price indexes rise appreciably. This popular corruption of the term inflation, originally defined as an increase in the money supply, makes it seem safe for the government to increase the money supply so long as the government's own price indexes do not rise noticeably. So, if these price indexes can somehow be kept down, the government can continue buying or allocating wealth which has been created by private individuals who must be satisfied with less than the free market value of their contributions.

---

[5] Figures from the Federal Reserve Bulletin, February 1965. Figures for the money supply include those for currency outside of banks, demand deposits, and time deposits of commercial banks which in practice may be withdrawn on demand.

## Price Rise Kept Down

Since World War II, there have been two continuing situations which have helped to keep official price indexes from reflecting the full effect of this huge increase in the money supply. The first such situation is that throughout this period American production of wealth has continued to increase. The second is that during these years foreigners and their banks and governments have taken and held off the market increasing supplies of dollars.

If there had been no upward manipulation of the money supply, the increased production of wealth would have resulted in lower prices. This would have provided more for everyone who earned or saved a dollar. It would also have reduced costs and increased the amount of goods and services that would have been sold at home and abroad.

As it was, with prices rising slowly over the 1945-64 period, the Federal government and our government-controlled banking system have been able to allocate the benefits of increased production, and a little bit more, to favored bank borrowers who pay lower than free market interest rates and those who received Federal funds over and above the sums collected in taxes or borrowed from private individuals or corporations.

Untold billions of dollars have also gone into the hands or bank accounts of international organizations, foreigners, their banks, and governments. Many of these dollar holders consider $35 to be worth more than an ounce of gold. Such dollar holders have felt they could always get the gold and, meanwhile, they can get interest by leaving their dollars on deposit with American banks. Foreign governments could even count such deposits as part of their reserves against their own currencies. For example, the more dollars held by the Bank of France, the more it can expand the supply of French francs. So the inflations of many European governments are built on top of the great increase in their holdings of dollars.

Short term liabilities of American banks to foreigners at the end of 1945 were only $6.9 billion.[6] By the end of last year, they had risen to an estimated $28.8 billion, an increase of $20.9 billion.[7] How many more dollars rest in foreign billfolds or under foreign mattresses cannot even be guessed. Should such foreign dollar holders lose confidence in the ability of their central banks to get an ounce of gold for every $35 presented to our government, more and more of these dollars will return to our shores where their presence will bid up American prices.

This whole process of increasing the money supply by semi-hidden manipulations is not only highly questionable from the viewpoint of morality and economic incentives, but it also has a highly disorganizing effect on the production pattern of our economy. Over the years, as these newly created dollars have found their way into the market, they have forced profit-seeking enterprises to allocate a growing part of production to the spenders of the newly created dollars, leaving less production available for the spenders of dollars which represent contributions to society. Once this artificial creation of dollars comes to an end, as it must eventually, those businesses whose sales have become dependent upon the spending of the newly created dollars will lose their customers.

---

[6] Federal Reserve Board "Supplement" to Banking and Monetary Statistics, Sec. 15. INTERNATIONAL FINANCE.

[7] FEDERAL RESERVE BULLETIN, February, 1965.

This will call for a reorganization of the nation's production facilities. Such reorganizations of business have become known as depressions. The depression can be short, with a minimum of human misery, if prices, wage rates, and interest rates are left free to reflect a true picture of the ever-changing demands of consumers and supplies of labor, raw materials, and savings. Private business will then move promptly and efficiently to employ what is available to produce the highest valued mixture of goods and services. Any interference with the free market indicators will not only slow down recovery but also misdirect some efforts and reduce the ability of business to satisfy as much human need as a completely free economy would.

The day of reckoning can only be put off so long. Once the nation's workers and savers realize that such semi-hidden increases in the money supply are appropriating a part of their purchasing power, they may take their dollars out of government bonds, savings banks, life insurance policies, and the like in order to buy goods or invest in real estate or common stocks, and even borrow at the banks to do so. If this trend should develop, the government would soon be forced to adopt sound fiscal and monetary policies.

The same effect might be produced by a rush of foreign dollar holders to spend the dollars they now consider as good as one thirty-fifth of an ounce of gold. In any case, an ever-increasing supply of dollars and ever-increasing prices will eventually bring on a "runaway inflation," unless the government stops its present practices before the situation gets completely out of hand.

The important thing to remember is that increases in the nation's money supply can never benefit the nation's economy. Such increases in the money supply do not and cannot increase the supply of goods and services that a free economy would produce. Such inflations of the money supply can only help some at the expense of others. Even such help for the politically favored is at best only temporary. As prices rise, it takes ever bigger doses of new money to have the same effect, and this in turn means still higher prices.

The fact is that no matter what the volume of business may be, any given supply of money is sufficient to perform all the services money can perform for an economy. All that is needed for continued prosperity is for the government to let prices, wage rates, and interest rates fluctuate so that they reveal rather than hide the true state of market conditions.

Under the paper money standard, politicians are easily tempted to keep voting for just a little more spending than last year, and just a little less taxing than last year. The gap can be covered by a semi-hidden increase in the money supply—just a little more than last year. Then, too, the illusions of prosperity are often helped along by an easy money policy—holding interest rates below those of a free market. This tends to increase the demand for loans above the amount of real savings available for lending. The banks then meet the demand for more credit by the bookkeeping device of increasing the bank accounts of borrowers.

Clever financial officials must then find ways to put off the day of reckoning. If gold continues to flow out, private travel, imports, and investments can be blamed and controls instituted. When the first controls do not succeed, more and more controls can be added.

When these fail, public attention can always be diverted by a war. War is now generally considered a sufficient excuse for more inflation and a completely controlled economy of the type Hitler established in Germany.

No man or government should ever be trusted with the legal power to increase a nation's money supply at will.

The great advantage of the gold standard is that gold cannot be created by printing presses or by bookkeeping entries. When a country is on the gold standard, politicians who want to vote for spending measures must also vote for increased taxes or sanction the issuance of government securities paying free market interest rates that will attract the funds of private savers and investors. Under a true gold standard, men remain free, the quantity of money is determined by market forces, and both the manipulated inflations and the resulting depressions are eliminated, along with all the poverty and human misery that they cause.

# Thought Questions

*(An excellent reference tool that may assist you in answering some of the following questions is Richard Maybury's book* WHATEVER HAPPENED TO PENNY CANDY? *(An Uncle Eric Book) published by Bluestocking Press, www.BluestockingPress.com*

1. What do business people do when they have more goods to sell than they have customers who are willing to buy at their asking price?

2. True or False. The way to move increased production into consumption is to adjust prices upward.

3. What is price? What is meant by a "just price"?

4. In a free market economy, do prices adjust to reflect consumer demand?

5. What is money?

6.  If the value of money is affected, will the prices of products and/ or services also be affected?

7.  Name and explain the three types of economic goods.

8.  What might happen to the price of oranges if a frost or freeze destroys the orange crop in Florida and California?

9.  Applying the example of loss from the Montreal apartment and war in "How Much Money," what were the losses from the attacks of September 11, 2001?

10. True or False. Any increase in the supply of money helps those who receive some of the new supply, but it hurts all those who do not. (A thorough explanation of this targeted supply of money can be read in Richard J. Maybury's book THE CLIPPER SHIP STRATEGY, published by Bluestocking Press, www.BluestockingPress.com)

11. True or False. Every time a government increases the money supply, it is taking wealth from some and giving it to others.

12. The article "How Much Money" appeared in THE FREEMAN in May 1965. In this article Pearcy Greaves stated, "The day of reckoning can only be put off so long. Once the nation's workers and savers realize that such semi-hidden increases in the money supply are appropriating a part of their purchasing power, they may take their dollars out of government bonds, savings banks, life insurance policies, and the like in order to buy goods or invest in real estate or common stocks, and even borrow at the banks to do so." An ambitious research project would be to determine how the nation's workers have invested their money since 1965.

13. Pearcy Greaves states that "once this artificial creation of dollars comes to an end, as it must eventually, those businesses whose sales have become dependent upon the spending of the newly created dollars will lose their customers." Is this what happened when the dot.com stock market plummeted toward the end of the 1990s?

14. Pearcy Greaves states, "Under the paper money standard, politicians are easily tempted to keep voting for just a little more spending than last year, and just a little less taxing than last year. The gap can be covered by a semi-hidden increase in the money supply—just a little more than last year. Then, too, the illusions of prosperity are often helped along by an easy money policy— holding interest rates below those of a free market. This tends to increase the demand for loans above the amount of real savings available for lending. The banks then meet the demand for more credit by the bookkeeping device of increasing the bank accounts of borrowers. Clever financial officials must then find ways to put off the day of reckoning. If gold continues to flow out, private travel, imports, and investments can be blamed and controls instituted. When the first controls do not succeed, more and more controls can be added. When these fail, public attention can always be diverted by a war." What do you believe the future economic outlook for the United States is at the time you read this article?

15. Pearcy Greaves says, "No man or government should ever be trusted with the legal power to increase a nation's money supply at will." Nikolai Lenin, Socialist founder of the Soviet Union said, "The best way to destroy the capitalist system is to debase the currency." Economist John Maynard Keynes said, "There is no subtler, or surer means of overturning the existing basis of society than to debase the currency. The process engages all the hidden forces of economic law on the side of destruction, and does it in a manner which only one man in a million is able to diagnose." Do you think you will learn enough about economics to increase the odds so that more than one person in a million can diagnose the hidden forces of economic law to help avoid the destruction to which Greaves refers? Explain your answer.

## What Do You Think?

1. **What is money?**

2. **What makes money valuable?**

3. **From where does money come?**

4. **What is paper money?**

5. **What materials are used to make U.S. coins today?**

# Eternal Love[8]

By Lawrence Noonan

*(for ages 14 and up)*

You are a member of the jury in this fictional court case.

The courtroom was hushed as the judge entered the chamber. It was crowded and many people could find standing room only. The trial, of course, had attracted nationwide interest and you could almost reach out and feel the expectancy.

The defendant, Charles Akins, was a rather small and timid looking man. Perhaps the timidity was a matter of fear—surely the somber courtroom and the overpowering majesty of the law were enough to inspire fear in a defendant. Mr.

---

[8] From THE FREEMAN, May 1960. Reprinted with permission of the Foundation for Economic Education, 30 S. Broadway, Irvington-on-Hudson, NY.

Akins certainly did not look like a criminal. As a matter of fact, he really looked quite respectable. But he did look frightened. And yet, there was determination there. And just a gleam of courage shining through, too.

Perhaps we should tell you now that the year was 1984. Not that there was anything so special about '84. Children went to school, grew up, worked, got married, and reared their own children. People went to church, voted, talked politics, argued, and endeavored to understand the subtleties of economics. But, all of it was just a little bit different. Especially in the way that people looked at things.

The Judge, the Honorable Warren Faber, having completed the preliminary ceremonies, was looking rather curiously, we thought, at the defendant.

"Mr. Akins," he said, "it is my understanding that you have retained no counsel and that you wish to defend yourself. Considering the gravity of the charge against you, I feel that you might like to reconsider."

"No, your honor," Akins replied, "I am going to defend myself."

"Mr. Akins, you are charged with a federal offense and are being tried in a federal court. You are charged with usurping the function of the government, of undermining and attempting to replace the monetary system of this country. With serious charges of this nature why will you not avail yourself of counsel?"

Mr. Akins seemed to be shivering slightly.

"Your honor, the facts have already been more or less determined. This is a matter of right or wrong. There isn't any legal thing involved here. I'm not guilty of anything. I simply want to tell what happened. I want to tell my story. I don't need any lawyer to do that."

The Prosecuting Attorney, Arnold Spear, leaped to his feet.

"Your honor, I object. The defendant is attempting to tell the court what is right and wrong. Further, I object to the statement that all of the facts are known."

"Objection overruled. This court will make its finding when the time comes. The defendant does have the right to represent himself. Mr. Akins, you have been sworn in. Now tell us what you consider to be your story."

"Well, this is the way it was. Back in 1957 my company, Trans-World Mining, became interested in increasing the market for our principal product—platinum. We had expanded our mining considerably and we needed more in the way of sales. We believed that platinum could be used far more extensively in jewelry and we bought a well-known jewelry manufacturing firm. We experimented with combining platinum with another metal, and we came up with something very beautiful and practical."

Judge Faber interrupted. "Mr. Akins, let me interrupt a minute. Up to this point you have simply told us that you were a mining company and had turned to the manufacture of jewelry from platinum?"

"Yes sir, that is correct. We had considerable success with the manufacture of jewelry, but as the years went by we began to notice a very unusual thing."

The Judge leaned forward intently. There was absolute quiet in the courtroom.

"We had manufactured small disk-like pieces of jewelry with some fine detail work on each side. Each piece had a small hole near one edge and we had intended them as pieces suitable for pendants. They sold for fifty, a hundred, and two hundred dollars apiece.

Frankly, we had not expected to sell too many of them. But as time passed, we began to experience something unusual. As I said, in the beginning, we didn't know how much to expect in the way of sales from a simple little piece like this. But as the years went by, the sales on this one small piece of adornment jewelry exceeded the sale of everything else the company was making! We couldn't understand it. These small pieces—originally priced at $50 to $200, and later at higher figures as the dollar price of platinum rose along with prices of everything else—were going like hot cakes. This went on and on. Finally, I had a market research outfit do a survey to find out why we were selling so many of these."

Charles Akins paused and licked his lips. The audience in the room was quiet but tense. Although they didn't have a doubt about the outcome of the trial, it was fascinating to hear this story from the man himself. After all, you didn't defy the government these days and get away with it!

Akins went on. "We discovered that people were buying these as an investment. People had become terribly afraid of the government's solvency. The government had issued barrels full of paper money. It wasn't even backed by gold any more. You couldn't even get gold."

Arnold Spear had jumped to his feet again. There was contempt in his eyes as he looked toward the defendant.

"Your honor, the defendant is beating about the bush. These things about paper money and gold are ridiculous! He's completely dodging the main issue—what was written on those coins?"

Little Mr. Akins was growing bolder.

"Your honor, it is my turn now to object. This was not a coin. We did not make these as coins. We did put an inscription on this piece of jewelry which conveyed—in a foreign tongue—Eternal Love. We had expected that this piece would be used for gift purposes. However, many people also interpreted this quotation to mean Eternal Value. Later on, this piece of jewelry began to be used by people in trade. They recognized and trusted the purity of its alloy. It had real value to them not only as an ornament but also as a medium of exchange. And as it came more and more into use in trade, this new use gave it still added value. People began saving them, hoarding them. We increased our production many times. We almost eliminated the manufacture of all other platinum items. The people wanted these. They were demanding them."

Akins paused again. He seemed to be either waiting to be challenged by the Prosecuting Attorney or for a request for clarification from the Judge. Nothing happened. Both the Judge and Arnold Spear had become absorbed in the story.

Akins proceeded now with growing confidence. He was on familiar ground. Regardless of the outcome, he had only one course and he followed it.

"Naturally, we were in business to make a profit. However, we, too, had become very apprehensive about the monetary situation and the government's policy. We finally decided that in addition to selling the platinum pieces, we would also make them the basis of our accounting and billing system—our private monetary unit. Thus, we began to use them as a medium of exchange. Of course, we were soon threatened by the Treasury Department. But they couldn't really do anything about it. Anyway, they didn't try. But later the value of the paper money in the country became almost worthless and they tried to blame Trans-World Mining for it. There was wild inflation. But the platinum pieces kept their value. People kept these whereas they would have kept gold if they could have gotten it. The government's paper money became almost worthless."

There was now both triumph and despair in Akins' voice.

"Well, it was almost incredible what had happened. The chaos became almost indescribable. People became frantic to get more of these platinum pieces. Where the value of paper money was going down and down, the value of the platinum piece was going up. It became the only sound means of exchange in the country."

Sadly he continued. "People came to realize that sound money was just as important as liberty itself. They found that there wasn't any honest freedom without honest money."

Another pause. "But now the government needs a scapegoat and they've got me. They want to put their own blame on someone else."

We won't bore you with the cross examination by Arnold Spear, the Prosecuting Attorney. He was eager for a conviction and the rhetoric thundered in the court. He likened Akins to one guilty of treason, of plotting the downfall of his own country. Akins was morally a leach and legally far worse. The thunder rolled on and on.

We don't know yet what the verdict is. The jury is still out.

## Thought Question

1. If you were a jurist, would you have found Mr. Akins guilty or not guilty of "usurping the function of the government, of undermining and attempting to replace the monetary system?" Before answering, read Article I.8.5 of the Constitution, which states: *"The people of the states empower the Congress to coin money and regulate the value thereof and also of foreign coins."* Also, before answering, read "Back to Gold" by Henry Hazlitt which appears on the next page. (Additional suggested reading: THE MAKING OF AMERICA: THE SUBSTANCE AND MEANING OF THE CONSTITUTION by W. Cleon Skousen, published by The National Center for Constitutional Studies, pages 420 to 426.)

## What Do You Think?

1. What is a gold standard?

2. Do you think a country's monetary policies should be tied to a gold standard?

# Back to Gold?[9]

by Henry Hazlitt

*(for ages 14 and up)*

In February of this year President de Gaulle of France startled the financial world by calling for a return to an international gold standard. American and British monetary managers replied that he was asking for the restoration of a world lost forever. But some eminent economists strongly endorsed his proposal. They argued that only a return to national currencies directly convertible into gold could bring an end to the chronic monetary inflation of the last twenty years in nearly every country in the world.

What is the gold standard? How did it come about? When and why was it abandoned? And why is there now in many quarters a strong demand for restoration?

We can best understand the answers to these questions by a glance into history. In primitive societies exchange was conducted by barter. But as labor and production became

---

[9] From THE FREEMAN, October 1965. Reprinted with permission of the Foundation for Economic Education, 30 S. Broadway, Irvington-on-Hudson, NY.

more divided and specialized, a man found it hard to find someone who happened to have just what he wanted and happened to want just what he had. So people tried to exchange their goods first for some article that nearly everybody wanted so that they could exchange this article in turn for the exact things they happened to want.

This common commodity became a medium of exchange—money.

All sorts of things have been used in human history as such a common medium of exchange—cattle, tobacco, precious stones, the precious metals, particularly silver and gold. Finally gold became dominant, the "standard" money.

Gold had tremendous advantages. It could be fashioned into beautiful ornaments and jewelry. Because it was both beautiful and scarce, gold combined very high value with comparatively little weight and bulk; it could therefore be easily held and stored. Gold "kept" indefinitely; it did not spoil or rust; it was not only durable but practically indestructible. Gold could be hammered or stamped into almost any shape or precisely divided into any desired size or unit of weight. There were chemical and other tests that could establish whether it was genuine. And as it could be stamped into coins of a precise weight, the values of all other goods could be exactly expressed in units of gold. It therefore became not only the medium of exchange but the "standard of value." Records show that gold was being used as a form of money as long ago as 3,000 B.C. Gold coins were struck as early as 800 or 700 B.C.

One of gold's very advantages, however, also presented a problem. Its high value compared with its weight and bulk increased the risks of its being stolen. In the sixteenth and even into the nineteenth centuries (as one will find from the plays of Ben Jonson and MoliÉre and the novels of George

Eliot and Balzac) some people kept almost their entire fortunes in gold in their own houses. But most people came more and more into the habit of leaving their gold for safekeeping in the vaults of goldsmiths. The goldsmiths gave them a receipt for it.

## The Origin of Banks

Then came a development that probably no one had originally foreseen. The people who had left their gold in a goldsmith's vault found, when they wanted to make a purchase or pay a debt, that they did not have to go to the vaults themselves for their gold. They could simply issue an order to the goldsmith to pay over the gold to the person from whom they had purchased something. This second man might find in turn that he did not want the actual gold; he was content to leave it for safekeeping at the goldsmith's, and in turn issue orders to the goldsmith to pay specified amounts of gold to still a third person. And so on.

This was the origin of banks, and of both banknotes and checks. If the receipts were made out by the goldsmith or banker himself, for round sums payable to bearer, they were bank notes. If they were orders to pay made out by the legal owners of the gold themselves, for varying specified amounts to be paid to particular persons, they were checks. In either case, though the ownership of the gold constantly changed and the bank notes circulated, the gold itself almost never left the vault!

When the goldsmiths and banks made the discovery that their customers rarely demanded the actual gold, they came to feel that it was safe to issue more notes promising to pay gold than the actual amount of gold they had on hand. They counted on the high unlikelihood that everybody would demand his gold at once.

This practice seemed safe and even prudent for another reason. An honest bank did not simply issue more notes, more IOU's, than the amount of actual gold it had in its vaults. It would make loans to borrowers secured by salable assets of the borrowers. The bank notes issued in excess of the gold held by the bank were also secured by these assets. An honest bank's assets therefore continued to remain at least equal to its liabilities.

There was one catch. The bank's liabilities, which were in gold, were all payable on demand, without prior notice. But its assets, consisting mainly of its loans to customers, were most of them payable only on some date in the future. The bank might be "solvent" (in the sense that the value of its assets equaled the value of its liabilities) but it would be at least partly "illiquid." If all its depositors demanded their gold at once, it could not possibly pay them all.

Yet such a situation might not develop in a lifetime. So in nearly every country the banks went on expanding their credit until the amount of banknote and demand-deposit liabilities (that is, the amount of "money") was several times the amount of gold held in the banks' vaults.

## The Fractional Reserve

In the United States today there are $11 of Federal Reserve notes and demand-deposit liabilities—i.e., $11 of money—for every $1 of gold.

Up until 1929, this situation—a gold standard with only a "fractional" gold reserve—was accepted as sound by the great body of monetary economists, and even as the best system attainable. There were two things about it, however, that were commonly overlooked. First, if there was, say, four, five, or ten times as much note and deposit "money" in circulation as the amount of gold against which this money had been issued, it meant that prices were far higher as a result of this more abundant money, perhaps four, five, or ten times higher, than if there had been no more money than the amount of gold. And business was built upon, and had become dependent upon, this amount of money and this level of wages and prices.

Now if, in this situation, some big bank or company failed, or the prices of stocks tumbled, or some other event precipitated a collapse of confidence, prices of commodities might begin to fall; more failures would be touched off; banks would refuse to renew loans; they would start calling old loans; goods would be dumped on the market. As the amount of loans was contracted, the amount of bank notes and deposits against them would also shrink. In short, the supply of money itself would begin to fall. This would touch off a still further decline of prices and buying and a further decline of confidence.

That is the story of every major depression. It is the story of the Great Depression from 1929 to 1933.

### From Boom to Slump

What happened in 1929 and after, some economists argue, is that the gold standard "collapsed." They say we should never go back to it or depend upon it again. But other economists argue that it was not the gold standard that "collapsed" but unsound political and economic policies that destroyed it. Excessive expansion of credit, they say, is bound to lead in the end to a violent contraction of credit. A boom stimulated by easy credit and cheap money must be followed by a crisis and a slump.

In 1944, however, at a conference in Bretton Woods, New Hampshire, the official representatives of 44 nations decided—mainly under the influence of John Maynard Keynes of Great Britain and Harry Dexter White of the United States—to set up a new international currency system in which the central banks of the leading countries would cooperate with each other and coordinate their currency systems through an International Monetary Fund. They would all deposit "quotas" in the Fund, only one-quarter of which need be in gold, and the rest in their own currencies. They would all be entitled to draw on this Fund quickly for credits and other currencies.

The United States alone explicitly undertook to keep its currency convertible at all times into gold. This privilege of converting their dollars was not given to its own citizens, who were forbidden to hold gold (except in the form of jewelry or teeth fillings); the privilege was given only to foreign central banks and official international institutions. Our government pledged itself to convert these foreign holdings of dollars into gold on demand at the fixed rate of $35 an ounce. Two-way convertibility at this rate meant that a dollar was the equivalent of one-thirty-fifth of an ounce of gold.

The other currencies were not tied to gold in this direct way. They were simply tied to the dollar by the commitment of the various countries not to let their currencies fluctuate (in terms of the dollar) by more than 1 per cent either way from their adopted par values. The other countries could hold and count dollars as part of their reserves on the same basis as if dollars were gold.

*Stop*

## International Monetary Fund Promotes Inflation

The system has not worked well. There is no evidence that it has "shortened the duration and lessened the degree of disequilibrium in the international balances of payments of members," which was one of its six principal declared purposes. It has not maintained a stable value and purchasing power of the currencies of individual members. This vital need was not even a declared purpose.

In fact, under it inflation and depreciation of currencies have been rampant. Of the 48 or so national members of the Fund in 1949, practically all except the United States devalued their currencies (i.e., reduced their value) that year following devaluation of the British pound from $4.03 to $2.80. Of the 102 present members of the Fund, the great majority have either formally devalued since they joined, or allowed their currencies to fall in value since then as compared with the dollar.

The dollar itself, since 1945, has lost 43 per cent of its purchasing power. In the last ten years alone the German mark has lost 19 per cent of its purchasing power, the British pound 26 per cent, the Italian lira 27 per cent, the French franc 36 per cent, and leading South American currencies from 92 to 95 per cent.

In addition, the two "key" currencies, the currencies that can be used as reserves by other countries—the British pound sterling and the U.S. dollar—have been plagued by special problems. In the last twelve months the pound has had to be repeatedly rescued by huge loans, totaling more than $4 billion, from the Fund and from a group of other countries.

## Balance of Payments

The United States has been harassed since the end of 1957 by a serious and apparently chronic "deficit in the balance of payments." This is the name given to the excess in the amount of dollars going abroad (for foreign aid, for investments, for tourist expenditures, for imports, and for other payments) over the amount of dollars coming in (in payment for our exports to foreign countries, etc.). This deficit in the balance of payments has been running since the end of 1957 at a rate of more than $3 billion a year. In the seven-year period to the end of 1964, the total deficit in our balance of payments came to $24.6 billion.

This had led, among other things, to a fall in the amount of gold holdings of the United States from $22.9 billion at the end of 1957 to $13.9 billion now—a loss of $9 billion gold to foreign countries.

Other changes have taken place. As a result of the chronic deficit in the balance of payments, foreigners have short-term claims on the United States of $27.8 billion. And $19 billion of these are held by foreign central banks and international organizations that have a legal right to demand gold for them. This is $5 billion more gold than we hold altogether. Even of the $13.9 billion gold that we do hold, the Treasury is still legally obliged to keep some $8.8 billion against outstanding Federal Reserve notes.

This is why officials and economists not only in the United States but all over the Western world are now discussing a world monetary reform. Most of them are putting forward proposals to increase "reserves" and to increase "liquidity." They argue that there isn't enough "liquidity"—that is, that there isn't enough money and credit, or soon won't be—to conduct the constantly growing volume of world trade. Most of them tell us that the gold standard is outmoded. In any case, they say, there isn't enough gold in the world to serve as the basis for national currencies and international settlements.

But the advocates of a return to a full gold standard, who though now in a minority include some of the world's most distinguished economists, are not impressed by these arguments for still further monetary expansion. They say these are merely arguments for still further inflation. And they contend that this further monetary expansion or inflation, apart from its positive dangers, would be a futile means even of achieving the ends that the expansionists themselves have in mind.

Suppose, say the gold-standard advocates, we were to double the amount of money now in the world. We could not, in the long run, conduct any greater volume of business and trade than we could before. For the result of increasing the amount of money would be merely to increase correspondingly the wages and prices at which business and trade were conducted. In other words, the result of doubling the supply of money, other things remaining unchanged, would be roughly to cut in half the purchasing power of the currency unit. The process would be as ridiculous as it would be futile. This is the sad lesson that inflating countries soon or late learn to their sorrow.

### The Great Merit of Gold

The detractors of gold complain that it is difficult and costly to increase the supply of the metal, and that this depends upon the "accidents" of discovery of new mines or the invention of better processes of extraction. But the advocates of a gold standard argue that this is precisely gold's great merit. The supply of gold is governed by nature; it is not, like the supply of paper money, subject merely to the schemes of demagogues or the whims of politicians. Nobody ever thinks he has quite enough money. Once the idea is accepted that money is something whose supply is determined simply by the printing press, it becomes impossible for the politicians in power to resist the constant demands for further inflation. Gold may not be a theoretically perfect basis for money; but it has the merit of making the money supply, and therefore the value of the monetary unit, independent of governmental manipulation and political pressure.

And this is a tremendous merit. When a country is not on a gold standard, when its citizens are not even permitted to own gold, when they are told that irredeemable paper money is just as good, when they are compelled to accept payment in such paper of debts or pensions that are owed to them, when what they have put aside, for retirement or old-age, in savings banks or insurance policies, consists of this irredeemable paper money, then they are left without protection as the issue of this paper money is increased and the purchasing power of each unit falls; then they can be completely impoverished by the political decisions of the "monetary managers."

I have just said that the dollar itself, "the best currency in the world," has lost 43 per cent of its purchasing power of twenty years ago. This means that a man who retired with $10,000 of savings in 1945 now finds that that capital will buy less than three-fifths as much as it did then.

But Americans, so far, have been the very lucky ones. The situation is much worse in England, and still worse in France. In some South American countries practically the whole value of people's savings—92 to 95 cents in every dollar—has been wiped out in the last ten years.

## Not a Managed Money

The tremendous merit of gold is, if we want to put it that way, a negative one: It is not a managed paper money that can ruin everyone who is legally forced to accept it or who puts his confidence in it. The technical criticisms of the gold standard become utterly trivial when compared with this single merit. The experience of the last twenty years in practically every country proves that the monetary managers are the pawns of the politicians, and cannot be trusted.

Many people, including economists who ought to know better, talk as if the world had already abandoned the gold standard. They are mistaken. The world's currencies are still tied to gold, though in a loose, indirect, and precarious way. Other currencies are tied to the American dollar, and convertible into it, at definite "official" rates (unfortunately subject to sudden change) through the International Monetary Fund. And the dollar is still, though in an increasingly restricted way, convertible into gold at $35 an ounce.

Indeed, the American problem today, and the world problem today, is precisely how to maintain this limited convertibility of the dollar (and hence indirectly of other currencies) into a fixed quantity of gold. This is why the American loss of gold and the growing claims against our gold supply are being viewed with such concern.

The crucial question that the world has now to answer is this: As the present system and present policies are rapidly becoming untenable, shall the world's currencies abandon all links to gold, and leave the supply of each nation's money to be determined by political management, or shall the world's leading currencies return to a gold standard—that is, shall each leading currency be made once again fully convertible into gold on demand at a fixed rate?

Whatever may have been the shortcomings of the old gold standard, as it operated in the nineteenth and early twentieth century, it gave the world, in fact, an international money. When all leading currencies were directly convertible into a fixed amount of gold on demand, they were of course at all times convertible into each other at the equivalent fixed cross rates. Businessmen in every country could have confidence in the currencies of other countries. In final settlement, gold was the one universally acceptable currency everywhere. It is still the one universally acceptable commodity to those who are still legally allowed to get it.

Instead of ignoring or deploring or combating this fact, the world's governments might start building on it once more.

# Thought Questions

1.  What is the gold standard and how did it come about?

2.  How long ago was gold first used as money?

3.  What is a banknote?

4.  What is the difference between a banknote and a check?

5.  Under what circumstances would an honest bank's assets remain equal to its liabilities?

6.  What is meant by payment "on demand" and why was this a problem for the first banks?

7.   When was the International Monetary Fund established and what was its purpose?

8.   What does a "deficit in the balance of payments" mean?

9.   What argument is put forth by advocates of a return to the gold standard?

10.   This article was written in 1965. As you read this question today, how many U.S. dollars does it take to purchase one ounce of gold?

11.   In 1964 the half dollar was 90% silver. In 1965 the money was debased. Five years later, how much silver was in a half dollar? (This will require research.)

12.   In what year did the first half dollars appear that contained no silver? (This will require some research.)

13.   In what year were Americans prohibited from using gold coins?

14.   If still posted online, read the article, titled "American Money: Past, Present and Future," originally published in THE FREEMAN, August 1976, Vol. 26, No. 8., at the following web address:

   http://www.libertyhaven.com/
   regulationandpropertyrights/bankingmoneyorfinance/
   americanmoney.html

15.   Review the "What Do You Think?" questions 1-5 that preceded the article "Eternal Love." How would you answer these questions now that you have read the article "Back to Gold?"

## What Do You Think?

1. Why might money become worth less or worthless?

2. What do you think the expression "Not worth a continental" means?

# Not Worth a Continental[10]

by Pelatiah Webster

*(for ages 16 and up)*

The fatal error—that the credit and currency of the Continental money could be kept up and supported by acts of compulsion—entered so deep into the minds of Congress and of all departments of administration through the states that no considerations of justice, religion, or policy, or even experience of its utter inefficacy, could eradicate it. It seemed to be a kind of obstinate delirium, totally deaf to every argument drawn from justice and right, from its natural tendency and mischief, from common sense, and even common safety.

Congress began, as early as January 11, 1776, to hold up and recommend this maxim of maniasm, when Continental money was but five months old. Congress then resolved that "whoever should refuse to receive in payment Continental bills, etc., should be deemed and treated as an enemy of his country, and be precluded from all trade and intercourse with

---

[10] First published December 13, 1780 in Philadelphia under the title "Strictures On Tender Acts." Reprinted with permission of the Foundation for Economic Education, 30 S. Broadway, Irvington-on-Hudson, NY.

the inhabitants . . ."—that is, should be outlawed, which is the severest penalty, except of life and limb, known in our laws.

## These Fatal Measures

This ruinous principle was continued in practice for five successive years, and appeared in all shapes and forms—in tender acts, in limitations of prices, in awful and threatening declarations, in penal laws with dreadful and ruinous punishments, and in every other way that could be devised. And all were executed with a relentless severity by the highest authorities then in being, namely, by Congress, assemblies and conventions of the states, by committees of inspection (whose powers in those days were nearly sovereign) and even by military force. Men of all descriptions stood trembling before this monster of force without daring to lift a hand against it during all this period. Its unrestrained energy ever proved ineffectual to its purposes, but in every instance increased the evils it was designed to remedy, and destroyed the benefits it was intended to promote. At best its utmost effect was like that of water sprinkled on a blacksmith's forge, which indeed deadens the flame for a moment, but never fails to increase the heat and force of the internal fire. Many thousand families of full and comfortable fortune were ruined by these fatal measures, and lie in ruins to this day, without the least benefit to the country or to the great and noble cause in which we were then engaged.

I do not mention these things from any pleasure I have in opening the wounds of my country or exposing its errors, but with a hope that our fatal mistakes may be a caution and warning to future financiers who may live and act in any country which may happen to be in circumstances similar to ours at that time.

## A Standard of Value

The nature of a Tender-Act is no more or less than establishing by law the standard value of money, and has the same use with respect to the currency that the legal standard pound, bushel, yard, or gallon has to those goods, the quantities of which are usually ascertained by those weights and measures. Therefore, to call anything a pound or shilling, which really is not so, and make it a legal standard, is an error of the same nature as diminishing the standard bushel, yard, or gallon, or making a law that a foot shall be the legal yard, an ounce the legal pound, a peck the legal bushel, or a quart the legal gallon, and compelling everybody to receive all goods due to them by such deficient measures.

Further, to make anything the legal standard, which is not of fixed but variable nature, is an error of the same kind and mischief as the others—for example, to make a turnip the standard pound weight, which may dry up in the course of a year to a pith of not more than two or three ounces, or to make a flannel string the standard yard, which will shrink in using to half its length. The absurdity of this is too glaring to need anything further said on it.

But to come to the matter now in question. The first observation which occurs to me is that the bills, which are made a tender, contain a public promise of money to be paid in six years. On which I beg leave to remark that the best and most indubitable security of money to be paid in six years, or any future time, is not so good or valuable as ready cash.

Therefore, the law which obliges a man to accept these bills instead of ready cash obliges him to receive a less valuable thing in full payment of a more valuable one, and injures him to the amount of the difference. This is a direct violation of the laws of commutative justice—laws grounded in the nature of human rights, supported by the most necessary natural principles, and enjoined by the most express authority of God Almighty. No legislature on earth should have (the) right to infringe or abrogate this freedom of choice in the exchange of goods for goods.

Again, the security arising from the public promise is not generally deemed certain. The public faith has been so often violated, and the sufferings of individuals thence arising have been so multiplied and extensive, that the general confidence of our people in that security is much lessened. Since a chance or uncertainty can never be so valuable as a certainty, those bills must and will be considered as less valuable than they would be if the security on which they depended were free of all doubt or uncertainty; and consequently, the discount of their value will always be estimated by, and of course be equal to, this difference. Therefore, the injustice of forcing them on the subject at full value of present cash is greatly increased.

These positions and reasonings are grounded on such notoriety of fact that any explanation or proof is needless; and I hope an objection against a law, drawn from the most manifest and acknowledged injustice of its operation and effect, will not be deemed trivial or be easily set aside or got over.

### An Honest Man

Suppose a man of grave countenance and character should, in distress, apply to his neighbor for the loan of 1000 silver dollars, with solemn promise on his honor and truth to repay them in a month, and in the meantime the Tender-Act under consideration should pass into a law, and the borrower, at the month's end, should tender 1000 of the new paper dollars in payment.

I beg leave here to ask of every member of the Assembly who voted for that law, and every other man who is a member of this state, what their sentiments of that action would be, and in what light they would view the borrower who tendered the paper dollars—that is, two-fifths of the debt[11]—in payment of the silver ones he had received: Would they consider him as an upright, honest man, or a shameless rascal?

In whichever of the two characters they may choose to consider such a man, it may be proper to note that the act in question, if passed into a law, would protect him, and not only so, but would subject the lender to the loss of the whole money if he refused to receive it. This is a somewhat delicate matter which it is painful to dwell long upon. I will therefore close what I have to say on it with a few very serious remarks, the truth, justice, and propriety of which I humbly submit to the reader:

1.  The worst kind of evil, and that which corrupts and endangers any community most, is that iniquity which is framed by a law; for this places the mischief in the very spot—on the very seat—to which every one ought to look and apply for a remedy.

---

[11] On March 18, 1780, the Continental Congress officially had recognized the debauchery of its currency, allowing it to exchange for specie at the rate of 40:1. By the time this piece was written, the unofficial exchange rate had further widened to 100:1. This probably explains Webster's illustration—"two-fifths of the debt."

2.  It cannot be consistent with the honor, the policy, the interest, or character of an Assembly of Pennsylvania to make a law which, by its natural operation, shall afford protection to manifest injustice, deliberate knavery, and known wrong.

3.  No cause or end can be so good—so heavenly in its origin, so excellent in its nature, so perfect its principles, and so useful in its operation—as to require or justify infernal means to promote it. By infernal means I mean such as are most opposed to Heaven and its laws, most repugnant to natural principles of equity which are all derived from Heaven, and most destructive of the rights of human nature which are essential to the happiness of society. Such laws are engraven by Heaven on the heart of every man. Some wicked men have formerly said, "Let us do evil, that good may come," whose damnation is just.

But perhaps this sort of argument may not have all the effect I could wish on the mind of every reader. I therefore proceed to another argument, which goes to the nature and principle of the act itself: The credit or value of money cannot, in the very nature of the thing, be supplied, preserved, or restored by penal laws or any coercive methods. The subject is incompatible to force; it is out of its reach, and never can be made susceptible of it or controllable by it.

The thing which makes money an object of desire—which gives it strength of motive on the hearts of all men—is the general confidence, the opinion which it gains as a sovereign means of obtaining everything needful. This confidence, this opinion, exists in the mind only, and is not compellable or assailable by force, but must be grounded on that evidence and reason which the mind can see and believe. And it is no more subject to the action of force than any other passion, sentiment, or affection of the mind; any more than faith, love, or esteem.

It is not more absurd to attempt to impel faith into the heart of an unbeliever by fire ... than to force value or credit into your money by penal laws.

## Trial and Error

You may, indeed, by force compel a man to deliver his goods for money which he does not esteem, and the same force may compel him to deliver his goods without any money at all. But the credit or value of the money cannot be helped by all this, as appears by countless examples. Plain facts are stubborn and undeniable proof of this. Indeed, this has been tried among ourselves in such extent of places and variety of shapes—and in every instance been found ineffectual—that I am amazed to see any attempt to revive it under any devisable form whatsoever. Countless are the instances of flagrant oppression and wrong, and even ruin, which have been the sad effects of these dreadful experiments, with infinite detriment to the community in general, without effecting in any one instance the ends intended. The facts on which this argument depends are fresh in everyone's memory.

I could wish, for the honor of my country, to draw a veil over what is past, and that wisdom might be derived from past errors sufficient to induce everyone to avoid them in the future. In conclusion, from the contemplation of the nature of the thing, and of the facts and experiments which have been made in every variety of mode and supported by every degree of power and exertion, it appears as plain and undeniable as intuitive proof that the credit or value of money is not in its nature controllable by force. Therefore, any attempt to reach it in that way must end in disappointment. The greater the efforts—and the higher the authority which may be exerted in that way—the greater must be the chagrin, shame, and mortification when the baseless fabric shall vanish into smoke.

## Natural Value

The only possible method then of giving value or credit to money is to give it such qualities, and clothe it with such circumstances, as shall make it a sure means of procuring every needful thing; for money that will not answer all things is defective, and has not in it the full nature and qualities of money. In this way only it will grow fast enough into esteem, and become a sufficient object of desire, to answer every end and use of money. Therefore, when the question is proposed: "How shall we give credit or value to our money?" the answer, the only true answer, is: "Bring it into demand, make it necessary to everyone, make it a high means of happiness and a sure remedy of misery." To attempt this in any other way is to go against nature, and of course into difficulty, only to obtain shameful disappointment in the end.

There is nothing better than to take things in their natural way. A great and difficult work may be accomplished by easy diligence if a good method and a wise choice of means are adopted; but a small work may be made difficult, very soon, if taken at the wrong end and pursued by unnatural means. There is a right and a wrong method of doing everything. You may lead with a thread what you cannot drive with whips and scorpions. The Britons have found this to their cost in the unnatural means they have pursued to preserve and recover their dominions in America. I wish we might be made wise by their errors. Happy is he who is made cautious by observing the dangers of others.

I would be willing to learn wisdom from Great Britain. It is right to be taught even by an enemy. Amidst all their madness, and in all their distresses for money, they never once thought of making their bank or exchequer bills a tender, or supporting their currency by penal laws. But these considerations may have little effect on some minds who are not very delicate in their choice of means, but seem resolved to carry their point, God willing or not.

I therefore hasten to another topic of argument. It appears to me the act is founded in mistaken and very bad policy, and by its natural operation must produce many effects extremely prejudicial to our great and most important interests.

It seems plain to me that the act has a fatal tendency to destroy the great motives of industry, and to dishearten and discourage men of every profession and occupation from pursuing their business on any large scale or to any great effect. Therefore, it will prevent the production of those supplies derived from husbandry and manufactures, which are essential to our safety, support, and comfort. Few men will bestow their labor, attention, and good money, with zeal, to procure goods and commodities for sale, which they know they must sell for money which they esteem bad, or at best doubtful.

The extent and dreadful effects of this are unavoidable and immense. If the industry of the farmer and tradesman is discouraged, and they cease to strive for large crops and fabrics, the consequence must be a universal diminution and scarcity of the produce of the country and of the most important articles of living, as well as commerce. The general industry of the country is of such vast importance — is an object of such magnitude — that to check it is to bring on ruin, poverty, famine, and distress, with idleness, vice, corruption of morals, and every species of evil. As money is the sinews of every business, the introducing of a doubtful medium—and forcing it into currency by penal laws—must weaken and lessen every branch of business in proportion to the diminution of inducement found in the money.

The same thing will render the procurement of supplies for the army difficult, if not utterly impracticable. Most men will hold back their goods from the market rather than sell them for money of a doubtful credit. There will be no possible way of collecting them but to send a superior force into the country and there take them by violence from the owner, which will occasion such an expense as will double the cost of the supplies by the time they get to the army, and be subject to a thousand frauds. This is the most obvious and natural operation of the act if we consider its own nature only, and it is confirmed by such ample experience, recent in the memory of every man, that it can leave no doubt but all this mischief must follow the act from its first operation.

## Bad Money Corrupts Men

I apprehend the act will, by its natural operation, tend to corrupt the morality of the people, sap the support, if not the very foundation, of our independence, lessen the respect due to our legislature, and destroy that reverence for our laws which is absolutely necessary to their proper operation and the peace and protection of society. Many people will be so terrified with the apprehension of seeing their real substance— the fruit of their labor and anxious attention—converted into a bundle of paper bills of uncertain value, that to avoid this evil they will have strong inducements to rack their invention for all devisable ways and methods of avoiding it. This will give rise to countless frauds, ambiguities, lies, quibbles, and shams. It will introduce the habit and give a kind of facility to the practice of such guile and feats of art as will endanger the uprightness, plain honesty, and noble sincerity which ever mark the character of a happy and virtuous people.

Many, who wish well to our independence and have many necessaries for our army which they would wish to supply, yet will be held back from offering their goods because of the doubtful value of the bills in which those supplies must be paid for. Instances of this sort I conceive will be so numerous as greatly to affect the supplies of our army and, of course, the support of our independence. The injuries and sufferings of people who are compelled to take said bills in satisfaction of contracts for real money will induce them in their rage to use the legislature, who formed the act, with great liberty and, perhaps, gross disrespect. The habit of reproaching the legislature and eluding the injurious act will become general, and pave the way to an habitual and universal abhorrence of our legislature and contempt of our laws, with a kind of facility and artful dexterity in eluding the force of the whole code.

I freely submit it to my readers as to whether these consequences are at all unnatural or ill-drawn, if the surmises are at all groundless, or the painting a whit too strong. No art of government is more necessary than that of keeping up the dignity and respectability of the legislatures and all courts and officers of government, and exciting and preserving in the hearts of the people a high reverence for the laws. And anything which endangers these great supports of the state ought to be avoided as a deadly evil.

## Bad Money Destroys Foreign Respect

The act, I apprehend, will give a bad appearance to our credit, honor, and respectability in the eyes of our neighbors on this continent, and the nations of Europe, and other more distant parts of the world. For when they learn that our own people must be compelled by the loss of half their estates and imprisonment of their persons to trust the public faith, they will at once conclude there must be some great danger, some shocking mischief dormant there, which the people nearest to and best acquainted with it abhor so much. And of course, as they are out of the reach of our confiscations and imprisonments, they will have little inducement to trust or esteem us.

Finally, the act will give great exultation and encouragement to our enemies, and induce them to prolong the war, and thereby increase the horrid penalty of imprisonment which is to last during the war. When they see that our money has become so detestable that it requires such an act as this to compel our own people to take it, they must at least be convinced that its nature is greatly corrupted and its efficacy and use nearly at an end. When we see the passionate admirers of a great beauty forced by lashes and tortures into her embraces, we at once conclude that she has lost her charms and has become dangerous and loathsome.

It cannot be fairly objected to these strictures that they suppose the bills funded by this act are of less value than hard money. The act itself implies this. The Assembly never thought of wasting time in framing an act to compel people to take English guineas, Portuguese joes, and Spanish dollars under penalty of confiscation and imprisonment.

I dare think that there is not a man to be found, either in the Assembly or out of it, that would esteem himself so rich and safe in the possession of 1000 of these dollars as of 1000 Spanish ones. The most effectual way to impress a sense of the deficiency of the act on the minds of all men, and even discover the idea which the Assembly themselves have of it, is to enforce it by penalties of extreme severity. For if there were no deficiency in the act it could not possibly require such penalties to give it all necessary effect, nor is it likely that the Assembly would add the sanction of horrid penalties to any of their acts unless they thought there was need of them.

The enormity of the penalty deserves remark. The penalty for refusing a dollar of these bills is greater than for stealing ten times the sum.

### Destroys Contracts and Credits

Further, the act alters, and of course destroys, the nature and value of public and private contracts, and this strikes at the root of all public and private credit. Who can lend money with any security, and of course, who can borrow, let his necessity and distress be ever so great? Who can purchase on credit or make any contract for future payment? Indeed, all confidence of our fellow-citizens in one another is hereby destroyed, as well as all faith of individuals in the public credit.

Upon the whole matter, the bills must rest on the credit of their funds, their quantity, and other circumstances. If these are sufficient to give them a currency at full value, they will pass readily enough without the help of penal laws. If these are not sufficient, they must and will depreciate and thereby destroy the end of their own creation. This will proceed from such strong natural principles, such physical causes, as cannot, in the nature of the thing, be checked or controlled by penal laws or any other application of force.

These strictures are humbly offered to public consideration. The facts alleged are all open to view and well understood. If the remarks and reasonings are just, they will carry conviction; if they are not so, they are liable to anyone's correction.

# Thought Questions

1.    Pelatiah Webster is credited by James Madison and others as having been the first advocate of _____.

2.    Webster's observations were written in the hope "that our fatal mistakes may be a caution and a warning to future financiers who may live and act in any country which may happen to be in circumstances similar to ours at that time." When and where was "Not Worth a Continental" first published?

3.    As early as January 11, 1776, Congress resolved that "whoever should refuse to receive in payment Continental bills, etc., should be deemed and treated as an enemy of his country, and be precluded from all trade and intercourse with the inhabitants . . ." Explain, in your own words, what this penalty means. How did it compare with other penalties of the day?

4.    Webster states, "No legislature on earth should have (the) right to infringe or abrogate this freedom of choice in the exchange of goods for goods." Illustrate the ways in which he believed the Tender-Act would infringe/abrogate this freedom.

5.    True or False. Webster states that, "The nature of a Tender-Act is no more or less than establishing by law the standard value of money . . . "

6.     Webster claims, "the thing which makes money an object of desire
       — which gives it the strength of motive on the hearts of all men
       — is the general confidence, the opinion which it gains as a
       sovereign means of obtaining everything needful." Does he believe
       that this confidence/opinion is compellable or assailable by force?
       Support your answer.

7.     According to Webster, what is the only true answer to the question
       "How shall we give credit or value to our money?"

8.     Why was Webster willing to learn wisdom from Great Britain?

9.     What did Webster believe the Tender-Act would do to industry?

10.    What affect did Webster believe the Tender-Act would have on
       the morality of the general public?

11.    According to Webster, how would the credit, honor, and
       respectability of America be viewed by foreign nations assuming
       the Tender-Act were instated?

12.    True or False. Webster believed the Tender-Act would destroy
       contracts and credits.

13.    True or False. The penalty for refusing one dollar of the new bills
       was greater than the penalty for stealing ten times that sum.

## What Do You Think?

1. What is deficit spending?

2. What are the pros and cons, if any, to minimum wage laws?

# The Gold Problem[12]

by Ludwig von Mises
*(for ages 16 and up)*

Why gold?

Because, as conditions are today and for the time that can be foreseen today, the gold standard alone makes the determination of money's purchasing power independent of the ambitions and machinations of dictators, political parties, and pressure groups. The gold standard alone is what the nineteenth century liberals, the champions of representative government, civil liberties, and prosperity for all, called sound money.

The eminence and usefulness of the gold standard consists in the fact that it makes the supply of money depend on the profitability of mining gold, and thus checks large-scale inflationary ventures on the part of governments. The gold standard did not fail. The governments sabotaged it and still

---

[12] From THE FREEMAN, June 1965. Reprinted with permission of the Foundation for Economic Education, 30 S. Broadway, Irvington-on-Hudson, NY.

go on sabotaging it. But no government is powerful enough to destroy the gold standard as long as the market economy is not entirely suppressed by the establishment of socialism in every part of the world.

Governments believe that it is the gold standard's fault alone that their inflationary schemes not only fail to produce the expected benefits but unavoidably bring about conditions that also in the eyes of the rulers themselves and of all of the people are considered as much worse than the alleged or real evils they were designed to eliminate. But for the gold standard, they are told by hosts of pseudo-economists, they could make everybody perfectly prosperous.

Let us test the three doctrines advanced for the support of this fable of government omnipotence.

### The Santa Claus Power of the State

The state is God, said Ferdinand Lassalle, the founder of the German socialist movement. As such the state has the power to "create" unlimited quantities of money and thus to make everybody happy. Irreverent people branded such a policy of "creating" money as inflation. The official terminology calls it nowadays "deficit spending."

But whatever the name used in dealing with this phenomenon may be, its meaning is obvious. The government increases the quantity of money in circulation. Then a greater quantity of money "chases," as a rather silly but popular way of talking about these problems says, a quantity of goods and services that has not increased. The government's action did not add anything to the available amount of useful things and services. It merely makes the prices paid for them soar.

If the government wants to raise the income of some people—e.g., government employees—it has to confiscate by taxation a part of some other people's incomes and to distribute the amount collected among its employees. Then the taxpayers are forced to restrict their spending, while the recipients of the higher salaries are increasing their spending to the same amount. There does not result a conspicuous change in the purchasing power of the monetary unit.

But if the government provides the money it wants for the payment of higher salaries by printing it, the new money in the hands of the beneficiaries of the higher salaries constitutes on the market an additional demand for the not increased quantity of goods and services offered for sale. The unavoidable result is a general tendency of prices to rise.

Any attempts the governments and their propaganda offices make to conceal this concatenation of events are vain. Deficit spending means increasing the quantity of money in circulation. That the official terminology avoids calling it inflation is of no avail whatever.

The government and its chiefs do not have the powers of the mythical Santa Claus. They cannot spend but by taking out of the pockets of some people.

## The "Cheap Money" Fallacy

Interest is the difference in the valuation of present goods and future goods. It is the discount in the valuation of future goods as against that of present goods. It cannot be "abolished" as long as people prefer an apple available today to an apple available only in a year, in ten years, or in a hundred years. The height of the originary rate of interest, which is the main component of the market rate of interest as determined on the loan market, reflects the difference in people's valuation of present and future satisfaction of needs. The disappearance of interest, that is an interest rate of zero, would mean that people do not care a whit about satisfying any of their present wants and are exclusively intent upon satisfying their future wants, their wants of the later years, decades, and centuries to come. People would only save and invest and never consume. On the other hand, if people were to stop making any provision for the future, be it even the future of the tomorrow, would not save at all and consume all capital goods accumulated by previous generations, the rate of interest would rise beyond any limits.

It is thus obvious that the height of the market rate of interest ultimately does not depend on the whims, fancies, and the pecuniary interests of the personnel operating the government apparatus of coercion and compulsion, the much referred to "public sector" of the economy. But the government has the power to push the Federal Reserve System and the banks subject to it into a policy of cheap money. Then the banks are expanding credit. Underbidding the rate of interest as established on the not-manipulated loan market, they offer additional credit created out of nothing. Thus they are intentionally falsifying the businessmen's estimation of market conditions. Although the supply of capital goods (that can only be increased by additional saving) remained unchanged, the illusion of a richer supply of capital is conjured up. Business is induced to embark upon projects which a sober calculation, not misled by the cheap-money ventures, would have disclosed as malinvestments. The additional quantities of credit inundating the market make prices and wages soar. An artificial boom, a boom built entirely upon the illusions of easy money, develops. But such a boom cannot last. Sooner or later it must become clear that, under the illusions created by the credit expansion, business has embarked upon projects for the execution of which it is not rich enough. When this malinvestment becomes visible, the boom collapses. The depression that follows is the process of liquidating the errors committed in the ecstasies of the artificial boom, is the return to calm reasoning and a reasonable conduct of affairs within the limits of the available supply of capital goods. It is a painful process, but it is a process of recovery.

Credit expansion is not a nostrum to make people happy. The boom it engenders must inevitably lead to a debacle.

If it were possible to substitute credit expansion (cheap money) for the accumulation of capital goods by saving, there would not be any poverty in the world. The economically backward nations would not have to complain about the insufficiency of their capital equipment. All they would have to do for the improvement of their conditions would be to expand credit more and more. No "foreign aid" schemes would have emerged. In granting foreign aid to the backward nations, the American government implicitly acknowledges that credit expansion is no substitute for capital accumulation through saving.

## The Failure of Minimum Wage Legislation and of Labor Unionism

The height of wage rates is determined by the consumers' appraisal of the value the worker's labor adds to the value of the article available for sale. As the immense majority of the consumers are themselves earners of wages and salaries, this means that the determination of the compensation for work and services rendered is made by the same kind of people who are receiving these wages and salaries. The fat earnings of the movie star and the boxing champion are provided by the welders, street sweepers, and charwomen who attend the performances and matches.

An entrepreneur who would try to pay a hired man less than the amount this man's work adds to the value of the product would be priced out of the labor market by the competition of other entrepreneurs eager to earn money. On the other hand, no entrepreneur can pay more to his helpers than the amount the consumers are prepared to refund to him in buying the product. If he were to pay higher wages, he would suffer losses and would be ejected from the ranks of the businessmen.

Governments decreeing minimum wage laws above the level of the market wage rates restrict the number of hands that can find jobs. They are producing unemployment of a part of the labor force. The same is true for what is euphemistically called "collective bargaining." The only difference between the two methods concerns the apparatus enforcing the minimum wage. The government enforces its orders in resorting to policemen and prison guards. The unions "picket." They and their members and officials have acquired the power and the right to commit wrongs to person and property, to deprive individuals of the means of earning a livelihood, and to commit many other acts which no one can do with impunity.[13] Nobody is today in a position to disobey an order issued by a union. To the employers no other choice is left than either to surrender to the dictates of the unions or to go out of business.

But governments and unions are impotent against economic law. Violence can prevent the employers from hiring help at potential market rates, but it cannot force them to employ all those who are anxious to get jobs. The result of the governments' and the unions' meddling with the height

---

[13] Cf. Roscoe Pound, Legal Immunities of Labor Unions, Washington, D. C., 1957, pg. 21.

of wage rates cannot be anything else than an incessant increase in the number of unemployed.

To prevent this outcome the government-manipulated banking systems of all Western nations are resorting to inflation. Increasing the quantity of money in circulation and thereby lowering the purchasing power of the monetary unit, they are cutting down the oversized payrolls to a height consonant with the state of the market. This is today called Keynesian full-employment policy. It is in fact a method to perpetuate by continued inflation the futile attempts of governments and labor unions to meddle with the conditions of the labor market. As soon as the progress of inflation has adjusted wage rates so far as to avoid a spread of unemployment, government and unions resume with renewed zeal their ventures to raise wage rates above the level at which every job-seeker can find a job.

The experience of this age of the New Deal, the Fair Deal, the New Frontier, and the Great Society confirms the fundamental thesis of British nineteenth-century liberalism: there is but one means to improve the material conditions of all of the wage earners, viz., to increase the per-head quota of capital invested. This result can only be brought about by additional saving and capital accumulation, never by government decrees, labor union violence and intimidation, and inflation. The foes of the gold standard are wrong also in this regard.

## U. S. Gold Holdings Shrinking

In many parts of the earth an increasing number of people realize that the U. S. and most of the other nations are firmly committed to a policy of progressing inflation. They have learned enough from the experience of the last decades to conclude that on account of these inflationary policies the ounce of gold will one day become more expensive in terms both of the currency of the U. S. and of their own country. They are alarmed and would like to avoid being victimized by this outcome.

Americans are forbidden to own gold coins and gold ingots. Their attempts to protect their financial assets consist in the methods that the Germans in the most spectacular inflation that history knows called "Flucht in die Sachwerte." They are investing in common stock and real estate and prefer to have debts payable in legal tender money to having claims payable in it.

Even in the countries in which people are free to buy gold there are up to now no conspicuous purchases of gold on the part of financially potent individuals and institutions. Up to the moment at which French agencies began to buy gold, the buyers of gold were mostly people with modest incomes anxious to keep a few gold coins as a reserve for rainy days. It was the purchases on the part of such people that via the London gold market reduced the gold holdings of the United States.

There is only one method available to prevent a farther reduction of the American gold reserve: radical abandonment of deficit spending as well as of any kind of "easy money" policy.

# Thought Questions

1.  Answer the question posed in von Mises' opening paragraph: "Why gold?"

2.  What is deficit spending?

3.  How does von Mises define the term: *interest*?

4.  What ideas did von Mises advance in each of the following subsections of his essay:
    a.  The Santa Claus Power of the State
    b.  The "Cheap Money" Fallacy
    c.  The Failure of Minimum Wage Legislation and of Labor Unionism
    d.  U.S. Gold Holdings Shrinking

5.  According to von Mises, what is the result of the governments' and the unions' meddling with the height of wage rates?

6.  What does von Mises propose as the "one method available to prevent a farther reduction of the American gold reserve?"

## What Do You Think?

1.  What is the difference between wants and needs?

2.  How would you put an end to unemployment?

# Jobs for All[14]

by Percy L. Greaves, Jr.

*(for ages 14 and up)*

Life is an unfinished series of wanting things. From the day we are born to the day we die, we want things we don't have. If we didn't, we wouldn't be normal human beings. We would have no reason to eat, work, or get married. All life is a struggle to satisfy more of our wants.

As our society is organized, the normal way to get more of what we want is to take a job. Then we can use the dollars we earn to buy more of the things we want for ourselves and our loved ones. Without a job, or a business of our own, we would all have to grow our own food and make our own clothes as well as anything else we wanted. Taking a job where we can use tools supplied by savers is the easiest way for most of us to satisfy more of our wants.

So most men want a job. To be without a job is most depressing. Continued unemployment, through no fault of one's own, is probably the darkest future any man can face.

---

[14] From THE FREEMAN, February 1959. Reprinted with permission of the Foundation for Economic Education, 30 S. Broadway, Irvington-on-Hudson, NY.

Such longtime mass unemployment is one of the great curses of our age.

The human misery, degradation, and moral temptation are not all. Besides these setbacks to the human spirit, there is the great unseen loss of the wealth the idle might have produced if they had been employed. This loss is shared by all. In a market economy every dollar holder can buy a share of the total wealth offered for sale. The greater the wealth produced and offered for sale, the more anyone can buy with each of his dollars. So we all have a stake in reducing unemployment and encouraging the production of more of the things men want most.

Yet millions of able and willing men have recently remained unemployed for months on end. What is the answer?

Let's use our heads. When we want to sell something, we sell it to the highest bidder. He buys it for the lowest price he can. That is what happens at auctions every day. It happens at the corn and cotton markets as well as the stock exchanges. Even the grocer with perishable fruits and vegetables reduces his prices until a highest bidder buys them.

That way, the seller gets the highest anyone is willing to pay, while the buyer pays the lowest price any seller will freely accept. Both buyer and seller get the highest possible satisfaction from every transaction. That is the way of the free market.

There is no reason why these same free market principles can't be applied to the services of working men. It would be very simple, requiring only two things. First, let every job seeker choose that job which offers him what he considers the best returns he can get for the services he has to sell. Second, let every prospective employer choose those job seekers who offer what he considers the best services he can get for the wages he can pay. Competition would soon see to it that no one was paid too much or too little.

Of course, such a simple solution would put an end to all privileges for those now overpaid. No union would then be able to hold up employers and consumers for more than they need pay in a free and competitive market. By forcing some wages above free market rates, some unions now get higher wages for their members than such workers would receive in a free society. But these forced higher wages for some mean that others must accept lower wages or unemployment (unless the government resorts to inflation). These lower wages and unemployment (as well as this pressure for inflation) would disappear if every man, including the unemployed, were free to compete for every job. As long as some of men's wants remain unsatisfied, there will be enough jobs to go around.

A free job market would provide "full employment" and greater production of the things men want most. Competition might drive down some dollar wage rates, but living standards would have to be higher. With more goods and services competing for every dollar, prices would be lower and everyone with a dollar would be entitled to a share of the increased production. Those now overpaid might temporarily suffer, but in the long run we would all be able to satisfy more of our wants.

With a free market in jobs, every man would be free to take the best offer available. Every employer would also be free to hire the applicants that pleased him most. No one would remain long unemployed. There would be jobs for all, more wealth produced, and a greater satisfaction of everyone's wants. What is more, the economic loss and dread of unemployment would evaporate.

# Thought Questions

1.    True or False. According to Greaves, life is an unfinished series of wanting things.

2.    Complete the sentence: As our society is organized, the normal way to get more of what we want is to _____.

3.    How does unemployment affect us in regards to wealth?

4.    What is the free market way for both buyer and seller to get the highest possible satisfaction from every transaction? Can these principles be applied to the services of workers? If so, how?

5.    The title of this article is "Jobs for All." Why does Greaves believe there should be jobs for all, and how does he propose this can be accomplished?

6.    What is the difference between wants and needs? Give examples.

## What Do You Think?

1. Do monopolies benefit or hurt the economy? Explain your answer.

2. What should be the role of government in controlling monopolies?

3. Should government try to encourage or curb competition among businesses? Explain your answer.

# Competition, Monopoly, and the Role of Government[15]
by Sylvester Petro
*(for ages 14 and up)*

In the free society government keeps the peace, protects private property, and enforces contracts. Government must do these things effectively, and it must do nothing else; otherwise, the conditions indispensable to personal freedom in society are absent. Whether or not a free society is attainable no mortal man can know; the limits of our knowledge are too narrow. But one thing we do know: that until at least the advocates of the free society are fully aware of the conditions necessary to its existence, it can never come about. For they must ever be on guard against new movements, ideas, and

---

[15] From THE FREEMAN, February 1974. Reprinted with permission of the Foundation for Economic Education, 30 S. Broadway, Irvington-on-Hudson, NY.

principles which would endanger its realization. And on the other hand, they must be sharply aware of existing impediments so that they may direct their energies intelligently to the removal of the causes of current imperfections.

I take up with considerable trepidation the task of arguing that government should quit trying to promote competition by means of the antitrust laws, especially since some proponents of the free society believe that vigorous enforcement of those laws is absolutely indispensable. Yet, antitrust laws are inconsistent with the basic principles of the free society, private property, and freedom of contract; they deprive persons of private property in some cases and outlaw certain contracts which would otherwise be valid. Moreover, they expand the role of government far beyond that envisaged by the theory of the free society and thus amount to an unconscious admission that the fundamental theory itself is incoherent; for antitrust policy implicitly accepts the Marxian premise that a laissez faire economy will result in the decay of competition and in the emergence of abusive monopoly. Finally, and this may be the most pressing reason for the present article, in their attempt to promote competition the antitrust laws may in fact be inhibiting it.

> *The great monopoly problem mankind has to face today is not an outgrowth of the operation of the market economy. It is a product of purposive action on the part of governments. It is not one of the evils inherent in capitalism as the demagogues trumpet. It is, on the contrary, the fruit of policies hostile to capitalism and intent upon sabotaging and destroying its operation.*
>
> **—Ludwig von Mises**
> HUMAN ACTION

## Vague and Uncertain Laws

One of the basic evils in the antitrust laws is the vagueness and uncertainty of their application. They have produced mainly confusion. Seventy some years ago the antitrust laws prevented the Great Northern Railway and the Northern Pacific from merging, although but a minor fragment of their respective lines overlapped in competition. But a few years later United States Steel was permitted to consolidate a vast preponderance of the steel production of the country under one management. Since then we have been off on another anti-merger binge, and so Bethlehem and Youngstown have been enjoined from doing on a smaller scale what U.S. Steel did on a grand scale. Socony and other integrated oil companies were told that they might not buy up distress oil at prices set in competitive markets. But only a few years earlier the Appalachian Coals Association had been permitted to act as exclusive marketing agent for most of the coal production of an entire region. Forty years after its foresight, courage, and capital had been instrumental in developing the great General Motors productive complex, the du Pont Company was ordered to give up control of its G.M. stock because of a relatively picayune buyer-seller relationship between them. Only space limitations preclude an almost endless listing of equally contradictory and inequitable results of the unpredictable eruptions from the antitrust volcano. At present, the allegedly competitive policies of the Sherman Act are mocked by those patently anticompetitive components of the antitrust laws, the Robinson-Patman Act and the fair-trade laws.

Thus, to the careful and honest observer the antitrust laws appear to be a charter of confusion, rather than the "charter of economic liberty" which oratory calls them. They have been transmogrified by the political vagaries to which their vagueness makes them susceptible into an insult to the idea that laws should apply equally to all. Some may regard these consequences as merely unfortunate incidents of a generally praiseworthy program. Yet we need continually to remind ourselves that law is for the benefit of the citizenry, rather than for the sport of government and of the legal profession. The main function of law is to provide people with clear and sound rules of the game, so that they may pursue their affairs with a minimum of doubt and uncertainty.

While aggravating the existing uncertainties of life, the antitrust laws can make no demonstrable claim to improving competition, despite the contentions of enthusiastic trustbusters. I have heard it said that the result of breaking up large firms is to create competition among its fragments, and thus to contribute to social well-being. But a moment's reflection will expose this as a bare and unsupportable assertion. Even though additional firms may be created by breaking up large businesses, the result is not necessarily in the social interest, nor does it necessarily create or improve competition. The social interest and competition are not automatically served by an increase in the number of firms. It is a commonplace that competition may be more vigorous and the service to society greater when an industry has few firms than when it has many. The question from the point of view of society is not how many firms there are, but how efficiently and progressively the firms—no matter how few or how numerous—utilize scarce resources in the service of the public. Maybe production will improve after a single large producer is split into fragments; but it is equally possible that it will not. No one can tell in advance, and it is also impossible to do so after the fact. The only thing that can be said with certainty about the breaking up of businesses is that government's power has been used to deny property rights rather than to protect them. If we really believe that private property is the most valuable institution of the free society, and that in it lies the strength of the free society, then it is wrong to abrogate that institution on the basis of pure guesswork.

## Monopoly Unionism

The antitrust approach to improving competition loses even more of its glamour when one understands that the most abusive and socially dangerous monopoly which exists today in this country is the direct product of special governmental privileges. Labor unions are today the most destructive monopolies in our system, and they are also the greatest beneficiaries of governmental special privileges.

First and foremost, there is the virtual privilege of violence, which trade unions alone enjoy. Neither individuals nor other organizations are so privileged. Memory is strangely short as regards union violence, and yet every big union in America has used it habitually, in both organizing and "collective bargaining."

Of the men who resist union membership, many are beaten and some are killed. They have much more to fear than do persons who reject the blandishments of sellers of other goods or services. And this is true despite the fact that the right not to join a union is as firmly entrenched in legal theory and the theory of the free society as is the right to buy as one wishes or to refuse to buy when one so wishes.

In 1959, the United Mine Workers engaged in one of its periodic purges of the nonunion mines which spring up continually owing to the uneconomic wage forced upon the organized mines by the UMW. An Associated Press dispatch, dated April 10, 1959, reported that "one nonunion operator has been killed, five union members charged in the fatal shooting, and three ramps damaged by dynamite since the strike began March 9. It has made idle more than 7,000 men over the union's demands for a $34.25 a day wage, a $2.00 increase." The grimmest aspect of the dispatch lay in the news that Governor A. B. Chandler of Kentucky was threatening—after a full month of terror and pillage by the union—to order National Guardsmen into the coal fields.

This is no isolated case. On the contrary, violence and physical obstruction are standard features of most strikes, except where the struck employers "voluntarily" shut down their businesses, in accordance with the Reuther theory of enlightened management which I have described in Power Unlimited: The Corruption of Union Leadership (Ronald Press, 1959). A special dispatch to The New York Times, dated August 5, 1959, reported that "a siege was lifted today for 267 supervisory employees at the United States Steel Company's Fairless Works here . . . . From now on the supervisory personnel will be allowed to enter and leave the plant at will for maintenance." The dispatch is silent concerning the probable consequence of any attempt by the steel companies to maintain production. But the fact that supervisors were besieged because of maintenance operations suggests that rank-and-file workers who attempted to engage in production would be mauled. It is not out of order to infer that the siege of the supervisors, otherwise a pretty silly act, was intended to get across that message.

The careful student of industrial warfare will discern a pattern of violence which reveals an institutionalized, professional touch. Mass picketing, goon squads (or "flying squadrons" as they are known in the Auto Workers union), home demonstrations, paint bombs, and perhaps most egregious of all, the "passes" which striking unions issue to management personnel for limited purposes—these are the carefully tooled components of the ultimate monopoly power of unions.

As a matter of fact, we have become so befuddled by, and so wary of, the terror, destruction, and waste of the unions' organizing wars that we view with relief and contentment one of the most prodigious contracts in restraint of trade ever executed—the celebrated "no-raiding pact" of the AFL-CIO. No division of markets by any industrial firm has ever achieved such proportions. The "no-raiding pact" divides the whole organizable working force in accordance with the ideas of the union leaders who swing the most weight in the AFL-CIO. It determines which unions are "entitled" to which employees. The theory of modern labor relations law is that employees have a right to unions of their own choosing. Reversing that principle, the "no-raiding pact" asserts that the choice belongs to the union leadership. If any business group were so openly to dictate the choices of consumers, it would be prosecuted by sundry federal agencies and hailed before one or another, or perhaps many Congressional committees. It would not receive congratulatory telegrams from the chief politicians of the nation. ꙅ𝓉ꝋℙ

## Government Intervention

The more one examines American labor law the more one becomes convinced of the validity of Professor Mises' theory that no abusive monopoly is possible in a market economy without the help of government in one form or another. If employers were permitted to band together peacefully in order to resist unionization, as unions are permitted to engage in coercive concerted activities in order to compel unionization, it is probable that the purely economic (nonviolent) pressures of unions would not be as effective as they have been in increasing the size and power of the big unions. But the government has taken from employers all power to resist unionization, by peaceful as well as by violent means. At the same time it has permitted unions to retain the most effective methods of economic coercion. And so picketing, boycotts, and other more subtle modes of compulsory unionism are in many instances as effective in compelling unwilling membership—in the absence of countervailing economic pressures from employers—as sheer physical violence.

Monopoly unionism owes much, too, to direct and positive help from government. Consider the vigorous prohibition of company-assisted independent unions which has prevailed for over twenty years. Although such small unions might at times best serve the interest of employees, the early National Labor Relations Board practically outlawed all independent unions, and more recent decisions continue to favor the big affiliated unions.

### The Majority-Rule Principle

But perhaps the most significant contribution of government to monopoly unionism is the majority-rule principle which makes any union selected by a majority of votes in an "appropriate bargaining unit" the exclusive representative of all employees in that unit, including those who have not voted at all, as well as those who have expressly rejected the union as bargaining representative. Majority rule is a monopolistic principle; it is always to be contrasted with individual freedom of action. But it is particularly prone to monopolistic abuse in labor relations. Determination of the "appropriate bargaining unit" is left to the virtually unreviewable discretion of the National Labor Relations Board. And that agency has in numerous instances felt duty-bound to carve out the bargaining unit most favorable to the election of unions. Indeed, politicians might learn something about gerrymandering from studying the unit determinations of the Labor Board.

Even if the gerrymandering could be eliminated, the majority-rule principle would remain a source of monopolistic abuse, based on monopoly power granted and enforced by government. A union may be certified exclusive representative in a 1,000-man bargaining unit on the basis of as few as 301 affirmative votes, for an election will be considered valid in such a unit when 600 employees participate. If a bare majority then votes in favor of the union, the remaining 699 are saddled with the union as their exclusive bargaining representative, whether or not they want it.

## Competitive Safeguards

Society has nothing to fear from unions which without privileged compulsion negotiate labor contracts and perform other lawful and useful jobs for workers who have voluntarily engaged their services. For they are then but another of the consensual service associations or agencies which a free society breeds so prolifically. Moreover, the free society has demonstrated that its fundamental mechanism, free competition in open markets, is tough and resilient enough to defend against exploitation by any genuinely voluntary association. The critical problem arises when a man or an association destroys society's chief defense mechanism by violent and coercive conduct, or when that mechanism is blacked out by special privilege from government. For then, without the checks and balances of free men vying against free men in civilized competition, society lies as prone to exploitation by the unscrupulous as a rich store would be without guards and burglar alarms.

When the sources and components of union monopoly are understood, it becomes clear that the antitrust laws cannot cure the problem. The fundamental source is to be found in failures and errors of government which the most elaborately conceived antitrust laws could not cure. The basic job of government is to keep the peace. It has not kept the peace in labor relations. Local, state, and federal governments have all failed to prevent labor goons and massed picket lines from interfering with the freedom of action of nonunion employees and of employers in bargaining disputes. (See my book, THE KINGSPORT STRIKE, Arlington House, 1967.) A similar failure in organizing campaigns has permitted unions which would be pygmies, if they represented only workers who wanted them, to become giants. The antitrust laws would equally clearly do nothing to remedy the monopolistic consequences of the positive aids granted by government to the big unions, such as the majority-rule principle and the virtual outlawry of small independent unions.

I am convinced that the socially dangerous aspects of big unionism have been brought about by the errors and failures of government which we have been considering. Government has on the one hand been tolerating the violence and economic coercion by means of which the big unions have attained their present power, and it has, on the other hand, positively intervened in their support. Moreover for the last forty years or more, officers of the national administration have played a critical role in the key industrial disputes which have set the pattern of the so-called inflationary wage-cost push.

The latter is a much more important fact than it may seem at first view. It suggests that the checks and balances of free enterprise are adequate to protect the public even from the artificially constructed compulsory labor monopolies which we now know. Moreover, it is not unreasonable to infer that those checks will work even more effectively if politicians not only stay out of negotiations but also enforce the laws against compulsory organization. These considerations suggest that the logical first step for those concerned about union power is to insist that government remove the present special privileges which unions enjoy and then wait patiently, to see if the program will work itself out without further government intervention.

### Government's Limited Role, As Outlined by Mark Twain

I believe that the same approach should be taken in respect to businesses suspected of monopolistic abuses. Rather than following the hit-or-miss political vagaries of the antitrust approach, it would be better to make sure that all special privileges, such as tariffs, exclusive franchises, and other governmental devices for blocking access to markets are withdrawn. Repeal of the tax laws which unfairly prevent high earners from amassing the capital necessary to compete with existing firms would also help much more than antitrust prosecutions do in promoting competition. In short, if government would confine itself to protecting property and contract rights, and if it would desist from impairing those rights, it would be doing all that government can do to promote competition. And we should not need to be greatly concerned about monopolies and contracts in restraint of trade. For, as Mark Twain's account of the career of the riverboat pilots' monopoly in the nineteenth century demonstrates, the free enterprise system is in itself fully capable of destroying all abusive restraints upon competition which are not supported and protected by government.

In the years before the Civil War, Twain writes in LIFE ON THE MISSISSIPPI, the river steamboat pilots formed an association which was to become, as Twain put it, "the tightest monopoly in the world." Having gone through many trials in building up its membership, a sudden increase in the demand for pilots gave the association its first break. It held members to their oath against working with any nonmember, and soon nonmembers began having difficulty getting berths. This difficulty was increased by the association pilots' safety record, which grew out of an ingenious method evolved by the association for current reports on the ever-changing Mississippi channel. Since the information in these reports was confined to members of the association, and since nonmembers had no comparable navigation guide, the number of boats lost or damaged by the latter soon became obviously disproportionate. "One black day," Twain writes, "every captain was formally ordered (by the underwriters) to immediately discharge his outsiders and take association pilots in their stead."

The association was then in the driver's seat. It forbade all apprentices for five years and strictly controlled their number thereafter. It went into the insurance business, insuring not only the lives of members but steamboat losses as well. By United States law the signature of two licensed pilots was necessary before any new pilot could be made. "Now there was nobody outside of the association competent to sign," says Twain and "consequently the making of pilots was at an end." The association proceeded to force wages up to five hundred dollars per month on the Mississippi and to seven hundred dollars on some of its tributaries. Captains' wages naturally had to climb to at least the level of the pilots', and soon the increased costs had to be reflected in increased rates. Then society's checks and balances went to work. This is Twain's summation:

"As I have remarked, the pilots' association was now the compactest monopoly in the world, perhaps, and seemed simply indestructible. And yet the days of its glory were numbered. First, the new railroad . . . began to divert the passenger travel from the steamers; next the war came and almost entirely annihilated the steamboating industry during several years . . . then the treasurer of the St. Louis association put his hand into the till and walked off with every dollar of the ample fund; and finally, the railroads intruding everywhere, there was little for steamers to do but carry freights; so straightway some genius from the Atlantic coast introduced the plan of towing a dozen steamer cargoes down to New Orleans at the tail of a vulgar little tugboat; and behold, in the twinkling of an eye, as it were, the association and the noble science of piloting were things of the dead and pathetic past!"

The moral: government's job is done when it defends the right of competitive businessmen or workers to take over functions which are being abused by monopolistic groups. The deeper moral is that monopolistic abuses rarely survive without a basis in one form or another of special privilege granted by government. The long steel, auto, and other big strikes we have suffered would not have lasted nearly so long if government had effectively protected the right of the companies to keep their plants operating and the right of employees to continue working during the strike.

# Thought Questions

1.  In a free society, what does Petro say the government should do (i.e., what are its jobs)?

2.  True or False. According to Petro, antitrust laws are consistent with the basic principles of the free society, private property, and freedom of contract. Support your answer.

3.  True or False. According to Petro, one of the basic evils in the antitrust laws is the vagueness and uncertainty of their application. Support your answer.

4.  What, according to Petro, is the most "abusive" and "socially dangerous" monopoly that exists today? From what does it result?

5.  According to Petro, how does the government intervene using monopoly unionism?

6.  What does Petro believe will happen without the checks and balances of free men vying against free men in civilized competition?

7.  What is the "logical first step" for those concerned about union power?

8.  True or False. "The free enterprise system is in itself fully capable of destroying all abusive restraints upon competition which are not supported and protected by government." Why?

9.  What is "the moral" of Petro's article?

# The Broken Window[16]

by Henry Hazlitt

*(for ages 12 and up)*

*Reprinted with Permission for Educational Use Only*

It is often sadly remarked that the bad economists present their errors to the public better than the good economists present their truths. The reason is that the bad economists are presenting half-truths. They are speaking only of the immediate effect of a proposed policy or its effect upon a single group. The answer consists in supplementing and correcting the half-truth with the other half.

But the lesson will not be driven home, and the fallacies will continue to go unrecognized, unless both are illustrated by examples. Let us begin with the simplest illustration possible: let us, emulating Bastiat,[17] choose a broken pane of glass.

---

[16] Clipping of Note No. 95 (FEE, 1959). Excerpted from ECONOMICS IN ONE LESSON (Harper, 1946). Reprinted here for educational use only with permission of the Foundation for Economic Education, 30 S. Broadway, Irvington-on-Hudson, NY.

[17] Frederic Bastiat, 1801-1850, French economist, statesman, writer.

A young hoodlum, say, heaves a brick through the window of a baker's shop. The shopkeeper runs out furious, but the boy is gone. A crowd gathers, and begins to stare with quiet satisfaction at the gaping hole in the window and the shattered glass over the bread and pies. After a while the crowd feels the need for philosophic reflection. And several of its members are almost certain to remind each other or the baker that, after all, the misfortune has its bright side. It will make business for some glazier. As they begin to think of this they elaborate upon it. How much does a new plate glass window cost? Fifty dollars? That will be quite a sum. After all, if windows were never broken, what would happen to the glass business? Then, of course, the thing is endless. The glazier will have $50.00 more to spend with other merchants, and these in turn will have $50.00 more to spend with still other merchants, and so ad infinitum. The smashed window will go on providing money and employment in ever-widening circles. The logical conclusion from all this would be, if the crowd drew it, that the little hoodlum who threw the brick, far from being a public menace, was a public benefactor.

Now let us take another look. The crowd is at least right in its first conclusion. This little act of vandalism will in the first instance mean more business for some glazier. The glazier will be no more unhappy to learn of the incident than an undertaker to learn of a death. But the shopkeeper will be out $50.00 that he was planning to spend for a new suit. Because he has had to replace a window, he will have to go without the suit (or some equivalent need or luxury). Instead of having a window and $50.00, he now has merely a window. Or, as he was planning to buy the suit that very afternoon, instead of having both a window and a suit, he must be content with the window and no suit. If we think of him as a part of the community, the community has lost a new suit that might otherwise have come into being, and is just that much poorer.

The glazier's gain of business, in short, is merely the tailor's loss of business. No new "employment" has been added. The people in the crowd were thinking only of two parties to the transaction, the baker and the glazier. They had forgotten the potential third party involved, the tailor. They forgot him precisely because he will not now enter the scene. They will see the new window in the next day or two. They will never see the extra suit, precisely because it will never be made. They see only what is immediately visible to the eye.

So we have finished with the broken window. An elementary fallacy. Anybody, one would think, would be able to avoid it after a few moments' thought. Yet the broken-window fallacy, under a hundred disguises, is the most persistent in the history of economics. It is more rampant now than at any time in the past.

## Thought Questions

1.  What is the "broken window fallacy?"

2.  In this article, Hazlitt uses the example of a broken window, a glazier, and a tailor to illustrate the "broken window fallacy." Can you think of other situations in which this fallacy may occur?

## What Do You Think?

1. If you had an idea for a new food product, what do you think you'd need to do in order to bring that food to consumers?

# Food from Thought[18]

by Charles W. Williams

*(for ages 15 and up)*

Important events in the exciting history of food have interesting, divergent, and often accidental beginnings.

In 1856 a boy in Pittsburgh grew some extra horseradish in his mother's garden. He borrowed a wheelbarrow, which he filled with bottles of ground horseradish and sold to local grocers. The boy was Henry Heinz; and from this first bottle of horseradish sauce grew the intricate worldwide business of the H. J. Heinz Company. Before 1900 that one variety had grown to 57, which today numbers close to 570 in this far-flung food empire.

In 1904 Thomas Sullivan, a tea merchant, sent samples of his various blends of tea to a few of his customers packed in little, hand-sewn silk bags. To his amazement, orders began pouring in by the hundreds for his tea put up in bags. His customers had discovered that tea could be made quickly without muss or fuss by pouring boiling water over tea bags

---

[18] From THE FREEMAN, November 1968. Reprinted with permission of the Foundation for Economic Education, 30 S. Broadway, Irvington-on-Hudson, NY.

in cups. Thus, quite by accident, was the start of a million-dollar innovation in the sale of tea.

In 1890 a salesman living in Johnstown, New York, while watching the time it took his wife to make some calf's-foot jelly, decided that powdering gelatin would save a lot of time in the kitchen. Charles B. Knox put his idea into operation, hired salesmen to go into peoples' homes to show how easily his gelatin could be dissolved in water and used. His wife worked out recipes for aspics and desserts to be given away with each package. This was the beginning of Knox Gelatine known today by every American housewife.

Peter Cooper, the inventor of the "Tom Thumb" locomotives, also invented a process for mixing powdered gelatin, sugar, and fruit flavors. This was fifty years before it began to appear on grocers' shelves as Jell-O. He was too early; merchandising methods had not been developed to convince housewives of the need for ready prepared foods. Just before the beginning of this century spectacular advertising for its day pointed out how many desserts could be prepared from this inexpensive, neat, clean package of Jell-O. Recipe booklets were distributed by the millions, as many as 15 million in one year, unheard of in that day. Another billion-dollar food business was launched.

Count Rumford, born in Massachusetts, who later migrated to England, was a leading physicist of the nineteenth century. He built the first kitchen range designed for use in a prison in Munich. This proved so efficient and workable that many wealthy people commissioned Count Rumford to replace their open hearth type of cooking apparatus with these new contraptions in their manor kitchens. By 1850 many American manufacturers had adapted Rumford's invention and were producing cast iron ranges in many sizes and shapes, lavishly decorated. From an experimental prison range, the modern stove industry was born.

In 1914 a young scientist from Brooklyn, New York, named Clarence Birdseye joined a scientific expedition to Labrador. He was also an avid sportsman, so he lost no time. He cut a hole in the thick arctic ice to try his hand at fishing. The fish froze as soon as they were exposed to the subfreezing air, often before he had them off the hook. To his surprise, the fish could be kept frozen for weeks and then defrosted and cooked like a fresh fish without any loss of texture or flavor. After returning to the United States, Birdseye made the same discovery while hunting caribou. The steaks from the quick-frozen caribou could later be broiled to a juicy, flavorsome rareness. Because of World War I, he had to drop many additional experiments in quick-freezing all kinds of food. After the war he went into the fishery business in Gloucester, Massachusetts, and experimented with fast freezing on the side. With a tremendous amount of good salesmanship, he raised money for the first quick-frozen food company. The first Birdseye package went on sale to the public in 1930. It would have been difficult to believe, at that time, that within a relatively few years almost every segment of our giant American food industry would be in quick freezing.

In Boston in 1894 a boardinghouse keeper was criticized by a sailor in her rooming house because her puddings were lumpy. Insulted at first, she became interested when he explained that the South Sea island natives pounded tapioca to a smooth consistency and suggested that she experiment by running some through her coffee grinder. Sure enough from there on her puddings were as smooth as silk. Soon she was putting up her finely ground tapioca in bags and selling them to her neighbors. She chose a very magic name—"Minute Tapioca"—and soon found a big business on her hands. Many quickly prepared foods have since copied the word "minute," but today a minute does not seem fast enough and has been replaced by "instant."

Many people wonder how the Aunt Jemima trademark began. Chris L. Rutt, with a partner, had purchased a flour mill. After some experimenting they developed a packaged pancake mix to use the flours they produced. Then one evening in 1889, Rutt attended a vaudeville show. There he got the idea for a name that reflected the festive spirit long associated with pancakes. A tune called Aunt Jemima, which accompanied a New Orleans style cake walk, inspired the name of the first ready pancake mix.

Chiffon cake was billed in huge cake mix ads in the 1940's as the "first really new cake in a hundred years." Harry Baker was a professional baker and owned a pastry shop in Hollywood, California. For years celebrities had flocked to his store and raved about his cakes. Many cooks feel that their personal recipes should be very valuable to some big food manufacturer but are shocked to find that variations of nearly every recipe have already been tried in the research kitchens. Harry Baker was one of the lucky ones; he sold his recipes for many thousands of dollars to General Mills. The valuable secret of his chiffon cake was that instead of shortening he used salad oil.

Going back many years to 1520, Cortez, the Spanish conqueror of Mexico, observed native Mayan Indians treating tough meat with the juice of the papaya, a common fruit in most tropical lands. He noted this in his writings about his conquest. Strangely enough, this find lay dormant until recent years, when the tenderizing element in papayas was turned into a powder, put up in jars ready to sprinkle on the surface of meat to make chuck and round steaks as tender as sirloin and porterhouse. From this long-forgotten idea came Adolph's Meat Tenderizer, a necessity in many homes.

In 1824 a German doctor living in Venezuela had a Spanish wife who had been sickly for years. Determined to cure her, he worked for over a year on a formula of herbs and spices until he invented a tonic that he claimed brought her back to health. Sailors stopping at the little port of Angostura found that this blend of herbs, spices, and the blossoms of the blue Gentian plant would cure seasickness. They spread the fame of Angostura bitters around the world, the process being speeded when they learned to add it to their ration of rum. When it became an essential part of a Manhattan cocktail, its place in our lives was further assured. Later, it was found to be an excellent addition in many food recipes, and today Angostura Bitters is found on almost everyone's food shelf.

Early traveling merchants from the city of Hamburg, Germany, learned from the Tartars in the Baltic Sea area how to scrape raw meat, season it with salt, pepper, and onion juice to make what is still called tartar steak. The people of Hamburg soon adopted the tartar steak. After many years some unknown Hamburg cook made patties out of the raw meat and broiled them brown on the outside and still pretty raw on the inside—a true hamburger. Today in the butcher shops of America, ground hamburger meat accounts for 30 per cent of all the beef sold to consumers.

The Toll House was a country inn in Massachusetts noted for good food. In the early 1940's Ruth Wakefield, who was then mistress of the inn, started serving a crisp little cookie studded with bits of chocolate. Miss Wakefield readily gave her customers the recipe, and all of a sudden, bars of semi-sweet chocolate began vanishing from the shelves of the stores in the area. It didn't take long for the Nestle Company, and later Hershey, to smoke out the fact that everyone was making the cookie recipe from the Toll House; and soon they were selling millions of packages of chocolate bits specifically so people could make these wonderful cookies. Today it is America's most popular cookie, available frozen, in ready-to-use cookie mixes, and already made in packages.

The early Chinese found that seaweed dried and ground into a powder and added like salt to food had a magical effect on meats and vegetables—all their natural flavor was enhanced. That's why Chinese food became so popular all over the world. Eventually our chemists discovered the flavor-enhancing element and called it glutamate. Today this product, monosodium glutamate, made from beet sugar waste, soy beans, or wheat, is a staple item in every market. It is known to American shoppers as Ac'cent.

Gail Borden, the son of a frontiersman, went to London in 1852 to sell a dehydrated meat biscuit at the International Exposition being held in England. He used all his money trying to put over his idea and had to travel steerage to get home. He was appalled at the crowded, miserable conditions imposed on the immigrant families coming to America. During the trip several infants died in their mothers' arms from milk from infected cows, which were carried on board most passenger vessels to furnish milk, cream, and butter for the passengers. Borden was sure there was a way to preserve milk for long voyages; but many before him had tried and failed, including Pasteur. After four years of intensive research, Borden perfected a process of condensing milk. In 1856 his patent was approved in Washington. After much work selling the idea to skeptics, the first canned milk was introduced to the American market and formed the cornerstone of the vast and diversified Borden Company.

In Battle Creek, Michigan, Ellen Gould White had a dream one night in which she was told by the Lord that man should eat no meat, use no tobacco, tea, coffee, or alcoholic beverages. As a Seventh Day Adventist she established the

"Health Reform Institute," a sort of sanitarium, where her guests ate nuts disguised as meat and drank a cereal beverage. This beverage was the creation of one of her guests named Charles William Post, who was suffering from ulcers. He named his beverage Postum. Post also invented the first dry breakfast cereal, which he called "Elijah's Manna." He decided to go into business producing his inventions; but the name Elijah's Manna ran into consumer resistance, so he changed it to "Grape Nuts."

In this same sanitarium was a surgeon named Dr. Harvey Kellogg, whose name along with Post's was destined to be on millions of cereal packages every year. One of Dr. Kellogg's patients had broken her false teeth on a piece of zwiebach, so he invented a paper-thin flake cereal from corn. Breakfast cereals immediately became a rage, and at one time there were as many as forty different companies in Battle Creek competing for this new health food business. So began the vast cereal business of today.

Margaret Rudkin was the wife of a stock broker and her son suffered from allergies. She made an old-fashioned loaf of bread from stone-milled whole wheat flour, hoping to build up her son's health. The bread helped her son; so her doctor persuaded her to bake the bread for some of his patients, and soon she was in business. When this bread was introduced in the thirties, it competed at 25 cents against the spongy white variety selling at 10 cents. Within 10 years, Maggie Rudkin's Pepperidge Farm Bread was in demand all over the East Coast and other bakers were making similar loaves—another small beginning for a nationally-known company, Pepperidge Farms.

One night Teddy Roosevelt, who had been visiting the home of President Andrew Jackson, stopped for dinner at the

Maxwell House, a famous eating place nearby. Roosevelt, a great extrovert, was so delighted with the coffee that when he finished he replaced the cup in the saucer with a formal gesture and cried out heartily, "that was good to the last drop," a phrase destined to make quite famous the coffee named after the Maxwell House.

St. Louis, Missouri, was the site of two important developments in the realm of food. In 1904 an Englishman was tending a booth at the St. Louis International Exposition demonstrating the virtues of a hot cup of tea. This was an insurmountable task during the hot July days in the Mid-West. Our Englishman, Richard Blechynden, disparagingly wiped the perspiration from his face as he watched the crowds pass him by. Finally, in desperation, he threw some ice into the hot tea urn and the crowds began to swarm around his booth. The drink was a sensation, and iced tea quickly became one of America's most popular thirst quenchers.

Still in St. Louis, but back in 1890, a physician ground and pounded peanuts to provide an easily-digested form of protein for his patients. The result was peanut butter, which was quickly and rightly adopted by food faddists all over the country. Today it is a staple found in almost every American kitchen. It's a rare mother who isn't thankful for healthful peanut butter when nothing else seems to tempt her children's appetites.

So, with these anecdotes, one can see that almost every great food company or food idea had a small but fascinating beginning. Some came quite by accident, others from diligent perseverance, reflecting the drive and ingenuity of the human race—free enterprise among free men.

# Thought Questions

1.  What is the main point Williams wishes to make in this article?

2.  Select three of the following food companies/concepts and, using information learned from this article, write a brief account of their origins:
    a.  H. J. Heinz Company
    b.  Tea bags
    c.  Knox Gelatine
    d.  Jell-O
    e.  Modern stove industry
    f.  Birdseye
    g.  "Minute" or "instant" foods
    h.  Aunt Jemima trademark
    i.  General Mills' chiffon cake
    j.  Adolph's Meat Tenderizer
    k.  Angostura Bitters
    l.  Hamburgers
    m.  Toll House cookies/chocolate chips
    n.  MSG (monosodium glutamate)
    o.  Canned milk/Borden Company
    p.  Grape Nuts
    q.  Breakfast cereals
    r.  Pepperidge Farms
    s.  Maxwell House's "Good to the Last Drop" slogan
    t.  Iced tea
    u.  Peanut butter

3.  If you answered the question that appeared at the beginning of "Food from Thought," then follow-up by contacting your county government offices. Tell them you are working on a school project and ask what must be done in order to distribute a food product to consumers.

## What Do You Think?

1. What would you do if you had a million dollars?

# Million Dollar Dream[19]

*(for ages 9 and up)*

I dreamed I had a million dollars and need never work again.

I thought of all the things I could now do because I had a million bucks. I would have the fanciest food money could buy. I would buy a fine house. Only the sportiest and most expensive automobile would suit me from now on. Clothing? Only the richest and finest would ever cover me again. Oh, I was in clover all right. My fondest wishes had come true.

In my dream I dressed and, being hungry, went to breakfast. There wasn't any. My wife was in tears. The food she had ordered the day before hadn't been delivered. Not even a bottle of milk or the morning newspaper greeted me when I opened the door. I tried to telephone the grocery but the line was dead. I said, "Oh, well, I'll take a walk and bring back something for breakfast."

The street was deserted. Not a bus, street car, or cab was in sight. I walked on and on. Nothing in sight. Thinking something had happened only to my neighborhood. I went

[19] From THE FREEMAN, March 1957. Reproduced by permission of The Employers' Association of Chicago. Reprinted with permission of the Foundation for Economic Education, 30 S. Broadway, Irvington-on-Hudson, NY.

to another. Not even a train was moving. Then people began to appear on the street—first, only a few, then many, then hundreds. I joined them and began asking questions: "What has happened? Where can I buy food?" Then I got the jolt. Somebody said, "Don't you know? Everybody has a million dollars and nobody has to work any more."

At first I was stunned. I thought that somehow a mistake, a ghastly mistake had been made—but there was no mistake. It was really true. Everybody had a million dollars and thought that work was over for him.

Then it dawned on me as never before that all of us are dependent upon all of the rest of us; that to a small extent at least my labor had a place, a part, in the total welfare of mankind. With an angry shout I tossed to the winds even the thought of a million dollars.

Then I woke up. My dream was over. The sun was shining, the birds singing, my wife rattling the breakfast things. I looked out the window and saw a world of people moving about their tasks, each contributing a little to my life and living, just as I contribute to theirs. I called to my wife, "Hurry up with that breakfast, sweetheart, I want to get to work."

*This fable, reproduced by permission of The Employers' Association of Chicago, illustrates that money is not wealth. Nor has it exchange value except as the owners and producers of goods and services find that it facilitates their trading with one another.*

*A society of nothing but consumers is indeed a dream that no amount of money can bring to realization. Anyone who attempts to issue money with no provision for its redemption in goods or services is due the same rude awakening that is in store for every dreamer of something for nothing.*

— **Bettina Bien Greaves**

# Thought Questions

1.  What is the "moral" or "lesson" of this story? In your answer, be sure to mention the concepts of: 1) wealth and money; and 2) producer and consumer.

2.  What do you think might happen if one person had all the money in the world?

    (NOTE: An excellent book, ALL THE MONEY IN THE WORLD by Bill Brittain, is out of print, but if you are fortunate enough to find a used copy, or a copy in a library, read what happens in this fictitious account of a young boy who wishes for all the money in the world.)

## What Do You Think?

1.  Do you believe government should protect its own citizens' businesses from foreign competition? Explain your answer.

# The Candlemakers' Petition[20]
### by Frederic Bastiat
*(for ages 15 and up)*

*(Paraphrased from the Original)*

We candlemakers are suffering from the unfair competition of a foreign rival. This foreign manufacturer of light has such an advantage over us that he floods our domestic markets with his product. And he offers it at a fantastically low price. The moment this foreigner appears in our country, all our customers desert us and turn to him. As a result, an entire domestic industry is rendered completely stagnant. And even more, since the lighting industry has countless ramifications with other native industries, they, too, are injured. This foreign manufacturer who competes against us without mercy is none other than the sun itself!

---

[20] Translated and slightly condensed by Dean Russell from SELECTED WORKS OF FREDERIC BASTIAT, VOLUME 1, Paris: Guillaumin, 1863, pp. 58-59. (Paraphrased from the original.) Reprinted with permission of the Foundation for Economic Education, 30 S. Broadway, Irvington-on-Hudson, NY.

Here is our petition: Please pass a law ordering the closing of all windows, skylights, shutters, curtains, and blinds—that is, all openings, holes, and cracks through which the light of the sun is able to enter houses. This free sunlight is hurting the business of us deserving manufacturers of candles. Since we have always served our country well, gratitude demands that our country ought not to abandon us now to this unequal competition.

We hope that you gentlemen will not regard our petition as mere satire, or refuse it without at least hearing our reasons in support of it.

First, if you make it as difficult as possible for the people to have access to natural light, and thus create an increased demand for artificial light, will not all domestic manufacturers be stimulated thereby?

For example, if more tallow is consumed, naturally there must be more cattle and sheep. As a result, there will also be more meat, wool, and hides. There will even be more manure, which is the basis of agriculture.

Next, if more oil is consumed for lighting, we shall have extensive olive groves and rape (variety of mustard) fields.

Also, our wastelands will be covered with pines and other resinous trees and plants. As a result of this, there will be numerous swarms of bees to increase the production of honey. In fact, all branches of agriculture will show an increased development.

The same applies to the shipping industry. The increased demand for whale oil will then require thousands of ships for whale fishing. In a short time, this will result in a navy capable of upholding the honor of our country and gratifying the patriotic sentiments of the candlemakers and other persons in related industries.

The manufacturers of lighting fixtures—candlesticks, lamps, candelabra, chandeliers, crystals, bronzes, and so on— will be especially stimulated. The resulting warehouses and display rooms will make our present-day shops look poor indeed.

The resin collectors on the heights along the seacoast, as well as the coal miners in the depths of the earth, will rejoice at their higher wages and increased prosperity. In fact, gentlemen, the condition of every citizen of our country— from the wealthiest owner of coal mines to the poorest seller of matches—will be improved by the success of our petition.

**To this Petition of the Candlemakers, Bastiat in effect replied:**

You neglect the consumer in your plea. Whenever the consumer's interest is opposed to that of the producer you sacrifice the consumer's—for the sake of increased work and employment. The consumer wants goods as cheaply as possible, even imports, if they are inexpensive. "But," you reply, "producers are interested in excluding cheap imports. Similarly, consumers may welcome free natural light, but producers of artificial light are interested in excluding it."

Nature and human labor cooperate in the production of commodities in various proportions, depending on the country and the climate. Nature's part is always "free." If a Lisbon orange sells in Paris for half the price of a Paris orange, it is because nature and, thus, free heat does for it what artificial and, therefore, expensive heat must do for the other. A part of the Portuguese orange is furnished free.

When we can acquire goods from abroad for less labor than if we make them ourselves, the difference is a gift. When the donor, like the sun in furnishing light, asks for nothing, the gift is complete. The question we would ask—and we pose it formally—is this: "Do you prefer that our people have the benefit of consuming free and inexpensive commodities? Or would you impose on them the supposed advantages of hard work and expensive production?"

*The author did most of his writing during the years before—and immediately following—the Revolution of February 1848. This was a period when France was adopting many socialistic policies. As a Deputy to the Legislative Assembly, Mr. Bastiat studied each interventionist measure and explained how it must inevitably hurt the people. Protective tariffs were his special target. He pointed out that "protection" gives a special privilege to certain producers. He showed how tariffs add to the cost of imports, and reduce competition from abroad, benefiting certain producers at the expense of other producers and of consumers who must pay the higher prices or go without.*

— **Bettina Bien Greaves**

# Thought Question

1.  What do you think of the logic of the candlemakers' petition? Do you agree with Bastiat's reply? If not, what would have been your reply? Keep in mind that the petition and answer were written in the mid 1800s. How do they relate to modern times? In answering, remember to keep in mind the principles of free market economics that you have learned from these articles.

## WHAT DO YOU THINK?

Answers to questions from "What Do You Think?" will vary and should be answered based on the reader's current knowledge and/or opinion of the topic. Questions should be answered before reading the article that follows each "What Do You Think?" section.

After reading an article, the reader should review his/her answers to the "What Do You Think?" questions to determine if the article has caused the reader to alter his/her thinking in any way. Why or why not?

## THOUGHT QUESTIONS

"Thought Questions" should be answered based on information learned from the article and/or further research. Opinions should be supported with research, examples, reason, and/or logic.

If you see the notation "Answers Will Vary" in the answer section that follows, this generally means that the student is required to answer the question using his/her own knowledge, experience, or intuition. In these instances, the educator should refer back to the chapter in the primary text to reference what the author said about the issue at hand compared to the student's answer; a "correct" answer should be thoughtful, complete, and on-topic.

# Answers

**A King of Long Ago**
1-10: Answers will vary.

**Not Yours to Give**
1. The Constitution (Article I.8.1) states, "The Congress shall have the Power To lay and collect Taxes, Duties, Imposts and Excises, to pay the Debts and provide for the common Defence and general Welfare

of the United States, but all duties, Imposts and Excises shall be uniform throughout the United States." For further reading about the interpretation of Article I.8.1, read pages 387-392 in THE MAKING OF AMERICA: THE SUBSTANCE AND MEANING OF THE CONSTITUTION by W. Cleon Skousen.

2. Answers will vary.

3. Horatio Bunce and Lawrence Reed would have agreed with each other.

4. According to the article, fire-insurance companies and capitalists will rebuild San Francisco.

5. Sockdolager: a heavy or knock-down blow.

6. Answers will vary.

7. Mr. Bunce is concerned that Congress will have no restraint on "charity." The lack of restraint could lead to fraud, corruption, and favoritism. Reader's opinions will vary.

8. Answers will vary.

9. Research exercise. Answers will vary.

10. Research exercise. Answers will vary.

**How Much Money?**

1. Business people might reduce the price of products to encourage customers to buy, or offer other incentives to spur sales.

2. False. The correct statement should be: The way to move increased production into consumption is to adjust prices downward.

3. Price, according to Richard Maybury in his book WHATEVER HAPPENED TO PENNY CANDY? is what a person wants in trade for what he has. A "just price" as used in this article, means a fair price, "reflecting the supposedly never-changing number of man-hours required for production."

4. In a free market society, prices adjust to reflect consumer demand.

5. Money is a commodity, the most easily traded thing in a society.

6. Yes, if the value of money changes, so will the value of products or services relative to the value of money.

7. The three types of economic goods are:
   a. Consumers' goods: goods that are valued because they supply satisfaction to those who use or consume them.
   b. Producers' goods: goods that are valued because they can be used to make or produce consumer goods.
   c. Money: good that is valued as a medium of exchange.

8. If the orange crop is destroyed in California and Florida, the price of any remaining oranges will increase because their supply is limited, assuming no increase in the money supply.

9. The losses from September 11, 2001 (also known as 9-11) include the loss of lives, the loss to the owners of buildings, the loss to insurance companies, the loss to the market society of the future services and contributions of those who were killed. The market society lost the contributions, temporarily, of those who were injured. The government supplied monetary compensation to families of 9-11 victims funded from taxpayer contributions. Human services and producers' goods were lost that were used to clear away the wreckage. If, or when, rebuilding occurs, the human services and producers' goods required to rebuild will also be lost to the market society. The diversion of goods and services to the 9-11 disaster means that the market will never be able to offer the things that such labor and goods could have otherwise been used to produce. With fewer things available to the market, prices will rise forcing each consumer to get along with less than would have been the case without 9-11.

10. True.

11. True.

12. Research project.

13. Richard Maybury, in his book THE MONEY MYSTERY, stated: "To end the 1982 recession, Federal Reserve officials injected tens of billions of dollars into the economy. To stop the 1987 crash and 1991 recession, they injected tens of billions more, and they did not stop. By 1997, the (stock) market had become the largest bubble in the history of the world (in terms of the number of people and amount of money involved)." When the dot.com bubble burst, many of those tech businesses dependent on the new money failed.

14. Answers will vary.

15. Answers will vary.

**Eternal Love**

1. Answers will vary.

**Back to Gold?**

1. Gold could be easily held and stored. It was beautiful and scarce. It was durable. It could be hammered or stamped into coins that had precise shapes and weights so that the value of other goods could be expressed in units of gold. Chemical tests could be conducted on

gold to determine that it was genuine. So gold became not only the medium of exchange, but also the "standard of value."

2.  Records show that gold was used as a form of money as long ago as 3,000 B.C. Gold coins were used as early as 800 or 700 B.C.

3.  Originally a banknote was an IOU from a bank, usually for gold or silver. Banknotes originated as receipts from vault holders issued as evidence that the gold or silver was on deposit with the vault holder for safekeeping and storage.

4.  If the receipts for gold or silver (held on deposit for safekeeping and storage) were made out by the goldsmith or banker himself for round sums payable to bearer, they were banknotes. If they were orders to pay made out by the legal owners of the gold themselves, for varying specified amounts to be paid to particular persons, they were checks.

5.  An honest bank did not issue more notes, more IOU's, than the amount of actual gold it had in its vaults. It would make loans to borrowers secured by salable assets of the borrowers. The banknotes issued in excess of the gold held by the bank were also secured by these assets. An honest bank's assets therefore continued to remain at least equal to its liabilities.

6.  Payment "on demand" means that depositors could request their money at any time without prior notice. The problem arose because the banks' assets, consisting mainly of its loans to customers, were usually payable only on some date in the future. The bank might be "solvent" (in the sense that the value of its assets equaled the value of its liabilities) but it would be at least partly "illiquid." If all its depositors demanded their gold at once, it could not possibly pay them all. An example of this can be seen in the film "It's a Wonderful Life" starring Jimmy Stewart when the depositors of Bailey Savings & Loan all demanded their money on the same day.

7.  The International Monetary Fund began in 1944. Representatives of 44 nations set up a new international currency system in which the central banks of the leading countries cooperated with each other and coordinated their currency systems through the International Monetary Fund. They agreed to deposit "quotas" in the Fund, only one-quarter of which need be in gold, and the rest in their own currencies. They would all be entitled to draw on this Fund quickly for credits and other currencies.

8.  A "deficit in the balance of payments" means the excess in the amount of dollars going abroad (for foreign aid, for investments, for tourist expenditures, for imports, and for other payments) over the amount

of dollars coming in (in payment for our exports to foreign countries, etc.).

9. Gold, as a basis for money, has the merit of making the money supply, and therefore the value of the monetary unit, independent of government manipulation and political pressure.

10. Answer can be found in the business / finance section of newspapers or via business reports on the radio, or by searching the Internet.

11. By 1969 a half dollar was 40% silver.

12. In 1971 the first half dollars entirely without silver appeared.

13. In 1933 domestic use of gold in America was prohibited.

14. Read the article.

15. Answers will vary.

**Not Worth a Continental**

1. James Madison and others credit Pelatiah Webster as having been the first advocate of a constitutional convention.

2. "Not Worth a Continental" was first published in December 1780, in Philadelphia, PA.

3. Answers will vary — Webster mentions that those who refuse to receive payment in Continentals will be treated as outlaws, which is the severest penalty (except for that of life and limb) known in the laws of their country/day.

4. Answers will vary. This is a summary of the article and should include reference to major points as outlined in section headers.

5. True. According to Webster, "The nature of a Tender-Act is no more or less than establishing by law the standard value of money..."

6. Webster does not believe this confidence/opinion is compellable/ assailable by force; he believes it must be grounded on evidence and reason that the mind can see and believe.

7. According to Webster: "Bring it into demand, make it necessary to everyone, make it a high means of happiness and a sure remedy of misery." (These are Webster's words; student responses may vary in wording, but should not vary in meaning.)

8. Webster wanted America to avoid the errors Britain had made. "Happy is he who is made cautious by observing the dangers of others. It is right to be taught even by an enemy."

9. Webster believed the Tender-Act would destroy the motives of industry and discourage people from pursuing their business on any large scale or to any great effort.

10. Webster believed the Tender-Act would tend to corrupt the morality of the people.
11. Webster believed the Tender-Act would present America in a negative way and might even induce enemies into war.
12. True. Webster believed the Tender-Act would destroy contracts and credits.
13. True. The penalty for refusing one dollar of the new bills was greater than stealing ten times that sum.

**The Gold Problem**
1. Answers will vary.
2. Deficit spending means increasing the quantity of money in circulation. That the official terminology avoids calling it inflation is of no avail whatever.
3. According to von Mises: "Interest is the difference in the valuation of present goods and future goods. It is the discount in the valuation of future goods as against that of present goods."
4. The ideas advanced by von Mises in each of the subsections of his essay are:  a) Government cannot spend but by taking out of the pockets of some people.  b) If it were possible to substitute credit expansion (cheap money) for the accumulation of capital goods by saving, there would not be any poverty in the world ... In granting foreign aid to the backward nations, the American government implicitly acknowledges that credit expansion is no substitute for capital accumulation through saving.  c) Governments decreeing minimum wage laws above the level of the market wage rates restrict the number of hands that can find jobs.  They are producing unemployment of a part of the labor force.  The same is true for ... "collective bargaining."  The only difference between the two methods concerns the apparatus enforcing the minimum wage...To the employers no other choice is left than either to surrender to the dictates of the unions or to go out of business.  d) There is only one method available to prevent a farther reduction of the American gold reserve:  radical abandonment of deficit spending as well as of any kind of "easy money" policy.
5. According to von Mises, the "result of the governments' and the unions' meddling with the height of wage rates cannot be anything else than an incessant increase in the number of unemployed."
6. According to von Mises, "(R)adical abandonment of deficit spending as well as any kind of 'easy money' policy" is the "one method

available to prevent a farther reduction of the American gold reserve?"

### Jobs for All
1. True. According to Greaves, life is an unfinished series of wanting things.
2. As our society is organized, the normal way to get more of what we want is to take a job.
3. Unemployment causes great unseen loss of the wealth the idle might have produced if they had been employed; the greater the wealth produced and offered for sale, the more anyone can buy with each of his dollars.
4. The free market way for both buyer and seller to get the highest possible satisfaction from every transaction is for the seller to sell to the highest bidder, and the buyer to buy at the lowest price he can. That way, the seller gets the highest anyone is willing to pay, while the buyer pays the lowest price any seller will freely accept. This concept can be applied to workers; first, every job seeker should choose that job which offers him what he considers the best returns he can get for the services he has to sell; second, every prospective employer should choose those job seekers who offer what he considers the best services he can acquire for the wages he can pay.
5. Answers will vary, but should include some of Greave's summative concepts from the final two paragraphs of his article.
6. Wants are things/services a person desires, but that are not necessary for survival. Examples will vary.

### Competition, Monopoly and the Role of Government
1. In a free society, Petro says the government should keep the peace, protect private property, and enforce contracts. It must do these things effectively and do nothing else.
2. False. Antitrust laws are inconsistent with these principles because they deprive persons of private property and in some cases outlaw certain contracts that would otherwise be valid.
3. True. According to Petro, one of the basic evils in the antitrust laws is the vagueness and uncertainty of their application. (Examples of support provided by Petro are found in the section of his article titled "Vague and Uncertain Laws.")
4. According to Petro, labor unions are the most destructive monopolies; they are a direct product of special governmental privileges.

5. Answers will vary.
6. Petro believes that society will be prone to exploitation by the unscrupulous — just as a rich store would be prone to exploitation without guards or burglar alarms.
7. The "logical first step" for those concerned about union power is to insist that government remove the present special privileges that unions enjoy and then wait patiently to see if the program will work itself out without further government intervention.
8. True: "The free enterprise system is in itself fully capable of destroying all abusive restraints upon competition which are not supported and protected by government." Why? Answers will vary.
9. Answers will vary. See Petro's final paragraph for guidance.

### The Broken Window
1. The "broken window fallacy" is thinking of only some of the parties involved in a transaction without considering others; seeing only what is immediately visible.
2. Answers will vary, but should remain consistent with the concepts in Hazlitt's story.

### Food from Thought
1. Charles Williams' main point is that each anecdote illustrates that almost every great food company/idea had a small but fascinating beginning and each reflects the drive and ingenuity of the human race — free enterprise among people.
2. Answers will vary.
3. Answers will vary.

### Million Dollar Dream
1. Answers may vary slightly but should highlight that (1) money is not wealth, and (2) it is impossible to have a healthy society in which there are only consumers and no producers.
2. Answers will vary.

### The Candlemakers' Petition
1. Answers will vary.

# Published by Bluestocking Press

## Uncle Eric Books by Richard J. Maybury

UNCLE ERIC TALKS ABOUT PERSONAL, CAREER & FINANCIAL SECURITY
WHATEVER HAPPENED TO PENNY CANDY?
WHATEVER HAPPENED TO JUSTICE?
ARE YOU LIBERAL? CONSERVATIVE? OR CONFUSED?
ANCIENT ROME: HOW IT AFFECTS YOU TODAY
EVALUATING BOOKS: WHAT WOULD THOMAS JEFFERSON THINK ABOUT THIS?
THE MONEY MYSTERY
THE CLIPPER SHIP STRATEGY
THE THOUSAND YEAR WAR IN THE MIDEAST
WORLD WAR I: THE REST OF THE STORY
WORLD WAR II: THE REST OF THE STORY

## Bluestocking Guides (study guides for the Uncle Eric books)
by Jane A. Williams and/or Kathryn Daniels

Each Study Guide includes some or all of the following:
1) chapter-by-chapter comprehension questions and answers
2) application questions and answers
3) research activities
4) essay assignments
5) thought questions
6) final exam

## More Bluestocking Press Titles

LAURA INGALLS WILDER AND ROSE WILDER LANE HISTORICAL TIMETABLE
CAPITALISM FOR KIDS: GROWING UP TO BE YOUR OWN BOSS by Karl Hess
ECONOMICS: A FREE MARKET READER edited by Jane Williams & Kathryn Daniels
BUSINESS: IT'S ALL ABOUT COMMON SENSE by Kathryn Daniels & Anthony Joseph

## The Bluestocking Press Catalog
Varied and interesting selections of history products: historical toys and crafts, historical documents, historical fiction, primary sources, and more.

**Order information:** Order any of the above by phone or online from:

### Bluestocking Press
Phone: 800-959-8586
email: CustomerService@BluestockingPress.com
web site: www.BluestockingPress.com